MEN OR INSECTS?

ALFRED FABRE-LUCE

MEN OR INSECTS?

A Study of Population Problems

Translated from the French by
ROBERT BALDICK

HUTCHINSON OF LONDON

HUTCHINSON & CO. (*Publishers*) LTD
178–202 Great Portland Street, London, W.1

London Melbourne Sydney
Auckland Bombay Toronto
Johannesburg New York

★

First published 1964

This book has been set in Times New Roman type face. It has been printed in Great Britain by The Anchor Press, Ltd., in Tiptree, Essex, on Antique Wove paper.

Table of Contents

Foreword 7

1 TOWARDS SATURATION 9

Merits and defects of statistics—Forecasts constantly outstripped—The decline in migration—The fall in mortality—The Ireland of yesterday and the China of today—Will they eat?—Towards a political unknown

2 TWO WORLDS 30

The underdeveloped countries: overpopulation as a cause of economic depression—Decreases in the birth-rate—Europe's past and future—The United States and its megalopolis—Dialogue between an optimist and a pessimist—Consequences of automation—'Demographic aggression'—Towards a metamorphosis?

3 THE INVESTORS IN MEN 55

Malthus and Marx—The practice of Communist countries—The Christian position—A new power: the demographers—A few sophistries refuted—Natalism on the Left

4 WHOM TO SUPPRESS? 76

Problems of old age—Euthanasia—Negative eugenics—A slight relief

5 BIRTH CONTROL 90

Margaret Sanger—A secret psychology—The 'pill'—Artificial and natural methods—Feminine ambiguities—Rivalry between pedagogues—Abortion in the East and the West—A world-wide desire for family limitation

6 A FEW GUIDING RULES 120

Hunger—An international aid strategy—Two sexual policies: Sweden and France—Birth control and the United Nations—The advance of leisure—The magic effects of numbers—A state of emergency

Notes 151

Bibliography 157

Foreword

A good many delicate matters are dealt with in this work. I have tried to treat them as I hope I have previously treated very different subjects: calmly, but without fear of facts or words.

It is impossible for me to name here all those who, from New York to Shanghai and from Delhi to Puerto Rico, have helped me in recent years in my study of demographic problems, but I would like to express my gratitude in a few particular cases.

First of all I wish to thank the civil servants, doctors, writers, research workers, and directors of private institutions with whom I came in contact in the United States. The old student that I am found in that country not only a mass of information which he would not have been able to collect anywhere else, but, at all times, friendly and effective assistance.

I would also like to express my gratitude to the members of the United Nations and Institut National d'Etudes Démographiques staffs who kindly permitted me to draw on their experience; to M. Alfred Sauvy, whose works I have always read with admiration even when I could not agree with their conclusions; to Dr. Lagroua Weill-Hallé, who allowed me to consult her with regard to certain present-day aspects of the French problem; and to Mlle Agnès Rondeau, who helped me to analyse a considerable body of documents.

A. F-L.

Hutchinson AND COMPANY

have pleasure in sending for review

MEN OR INSECTS?

Alfred Fabre-Luce 21s

Publication date: 2.3.64.

The publishers request that no review should appear before the publication date and would be glad to receive a copy of the issue containing a notice or review. Further information about this book or its author will gladly be given by the Publicity Manager (LANgham 3020).

HUTCHINSON & CO (PUBLISHERS) LTD
178–202 Gt Portland St. London W1

One

TOWARDS SATURATION

IN THE course of preparing this work I read a great many statistics. I was going to say that I found them as exciting as a novel. But the comparison would be deceptive, for present-day novels are often boring, whereas figures become more and more interesting. As the number of calculations increases (and mankind becomes more uniform) they approximate more closely to reality. Until recently they merely allowed us to establish with a certain time-lag static pictures, rather like the patiently arranged poses of the photographers of old. We now know how to take snapshots. Thanks to electronic machines, we can witness transformations as they are occurring. We see human masses slipping past us like glaciers—or rather, for some time past, like avalanches. We register competitions of which, a little while ago, we had no idea. (While I have been writing these lines South America has just beaten North America by a short head, by passing the winning-post of 200 million inhabitants just before her.)

Through the medium of demographic statistics men deprived of all other means of expression utter cries of distress, inform the well fed that they are hungry, the well housed that they are living in a single room with unwanted children. Certain statistics denounce in a collective, anonymous form crimes of which not a single one has been separately admitted. In several regions of Asia boys and girls, in comparable numbers at birth, form two perceptibly unequal groups a few years later. The parents have not slit their daughters' throats; they have simply neglected them. In Sparta and Athens, 2,500 years ago, surplus children were exposed to the elements: that was a way of relieving the family while leaving the victims a slight chance of survival. We had imagined that this custom had disappeared. Present-day censuses show that it is still discreetly alive.

Other statistics are proud proclamations of anarchy. It was Christian countries, accustomed to repeating the Bible's dictum: 'Increase and multiply'—Sweden, France, Britain—which were the first to set the example of voluntary birth control. On the other hand, although the Koran lays down no prohibitions on the subject, contraception has never so far been practised in Moslem countries. Mussolini had asked the Italians to have more children. The Italians answered him by dropping the national birth-rate from 27 per 1,000 in 1925–9 to 23 per 1,000 in 1935–9. Spain since 1939 has had a regime which is conservative and Catholic, and therefore in favour of a high birth-rate. The birth-rate has none the less dropped from 27 per 1,000 in 1930–5 (before the Civil War) to 20 per 1,000 in 1950–4, a figure well below that of the United States, a largely Protestant country and the bastion of birth control. These figures, like rays which can pass through walls, show us disciplined citizens and pious believers disobeying in the privacy of their beds the orders of the temporal or spiritual powers-that-be.[1]

The distribution of population by age is nowadays shown by means of diagrams or superimposed rectangles representing the different groups. In the underdeveloped countries, with a high birth-rate and premature mortality, these constructions look like Mayan pyramids: the rectangles, very wide at the base, grow rapidly smaller. Industrial civilization produces new shapes which have a narrower base (voluntarily restricted births) and rise almost vertically at first, on account of the low mortality of children and adults. The height of the construction remains limited, all the same, for modern medicine prolongs life only within fairly narrow bounds (the century). Thus, the longer deaths are delayed, the more abruptly they occur. At the approach of the inexorable term a sudden incurvation is produced. The pyramid has become an inverted saucer.

In periods of stress and turmoil irregularities appear. Then the shape on the graph looks more like a tree which has been pruned by wars but afterwards throws out its branches (the compensating births of post-war periods) all the more vigorously. The precision of the diagram produces a *true* picture. This picture informs to an equal degree the artist who interprets it figuratively and the scientist who takes it at its abstract value. Looking at it, both could roughly reconstruct a story of which they knew nothing, and would assign the right dates to the great political cataclysms and medical revolutions. Only half a century ago they would have hesitated to interpret certain narrowings, which might have been due to war or epidemic. The two scourges sometimes coincided, the former attracting the latter. Spanish influenza and the French campaign combined to swell the mortality of 1918. But nowadays the great human catastrophes are nearly always the work of man. The latest to date is the growth of population itself. For, as we shall see, the multiplication of mankind is tending to become self-destructive.

People are beginning to realize this, with the result that the publication of a statistical figure sometimes assumes the proportions of a big political event. When in 1930 I went to see the Chinese Foreign Minister at Nanking, he did not know, to within 100 million, the population of his country. This was still true of his successor in 1950. The 1953 census, which counted more than 600 million Chinese, gave Mao Tse Tung a shock which persuaded him to try to put a brake on this growth. Similarly the Indian census of 1961 has just given a lively stimulus to Nehru's birth-control policy. Only a few years ago a child in the Far East was born, as far as we were concerned, in another world. His own fellow countrymen, except within the narrow family circle, were not informed of his appearance. Today he preoccupies us all. This new-born child joins a mass which is growing from one moment to the next. We, on the other hand—we Englishmen and

Frenchmen, we Westerners, we Whites—have a feeling that we are shrinking.

Everywhere the spread of demographic statistics is inducing men to consider from a civic point of view the most intimate event in their private life. Yesterday they alone made decisions about their posterity. Or rather they allowed chance to make the decisions for them. Now they have the feeling of being responsible for the future of mankind. The act of reproduction has become deliberate, *political*. The animal in man has scarcely changed, but the mind which controls it is on the alert.

For a long time now, in the developed countries, there has been a link between the birth-rate and economic conditions. In Prussia, as far back as the eighteenth century, the figures for births followed, year by year, the figures for the harvests. In England the launching of the campaign for birth control dates back to the economic crisis of 1870–80, and the rise in the birth-rate after the last war accompanied the triumph of the policy of full employment. There have always been many women who have decided the question of their posterity in accordance with social conditions. The fear of ostracism (in the case of an illegitimate child) or of shortage of money (in the families of unemployed workers) induces them to forestall or interrupt their pregnancies. Inversely, greater tolerance with regard to unmarried mothers, family allowances, and unemployment benefits encourage them to have children.

At a certain moment in pregnancy the embryo turns over in the mother's womb to place itself head-down facing the exit. A sociologist might imagine that the newcomer, learning that circumstances outside are favourable, is deciding to take the plunge. He is not entering a natural world but an organized society. He is a future taxpayer, a future national serviceman, a future elector. Consequently the news of his arrival is announced to all his fellows, sometimes in spectacular fashion. In Washington, at the Ministry of Health, a light flashes every seven seconds to announce the arrival of an American baby.

You may resist this intrusion and say: 'I don't want to know about those Chinese or American babies. I am interested only in my own and I intend to follow my own sweet will.' But your own sweet will is no surprise to the demographer. He knows you, if not individually, at least as a social unit. Although every suicide has its individual motive, there is an annual scale of suicides and a fairly constant connection between the suicide figures in different countries. There are even relatively coherent birth-rate curves. These do not merely register your actions: they help to determine them. Soon, precisely because of their diffusion, they may well allow us to make satisfactory predictions.

For these reasons, and for many others too, I find statistics tremendously interesting. But we must not expect more of them than they can give. On a good many underdeveloped countries (precisely those where the gravest problems of overpopulation occur) we possess only inadequate information. Governments publish statistics which are contradicted by sample surveys. 'Only fifty per cent of births are registered', says the United Nations demographic year-book; but this statement is itself misleading. (It is not enough to double the number of registered births to have the number of actual births.) As for the distant past, we have no reliable bases on which to work. I none the less find, fairly often, in ostensibly 'scientific' works, estimates of the world's population in the Middle Ages or even at the beginning of history. In such cases the use of figures is simply a bluff by which ignorant human beings are trying to impress other ignorant human beings who are at least superior to them in that they do not *claim* to be knowledgeable.

In Communist countries statistics are so essential to the regime that they ought to be given special attention. Yet it is in those countries that statistics tell the biggest lies. Between 1950 and 1955 the U.S.S.R. credited itself with twenty million imaginary Russians. It then decided to correct the record. It therefore dropped all at once (retrospectively) from 200 million inhabitants to 180 million. Had the Russians wanted to hide from the world the state of demographic weakness in which the German invasion had left them, and the extent of mortality in the labour camps after the end of hostilities? Or had they simply got their figures wrong as a result of the chaos created by the war? I cannot say. But it is amusing to find such vague approximations in a country where the man in the street knows the number of underground stations in Moscow and suspects the French tourist who cannot immediately quote the number of stations on the Paris Métro of trying to conceal an inferiority in his country.

In China it is far worse. A few weeks before the date by which the 1953 census was due to be completed it had scarcely begun. The operation was accordingly speeded up: some citizens were counted twice, others were forgotten, and the number of inhabitants in desert regions was arrived at by guesswork. Mao Tse Tung none the less produced some statistics which appeared to be very precise, and which included an item of 3,384 centenarians and a special section devoted to a solitary old man aged 155. Since then there have been no more censuses, but figures which do not tally have been published for population growth and the birth-rate. So much for the population. When it comes to food resources the statistics are not just vague but positively mad. In 1958, a few months after announcing that the year's harvest had produced a record figure of 375 million tons of cereals, the Central Committee of the Communist Party reduced this figure to 250 million. An astounding correction, yet one which the experts considered inadequate. Had there been, at the summit, a deliberate attempt to deceive? That is not certain. The incident probably enables us to diagnose a more deep-seated ailment of the Communist regime. Hoping to receive from its agents figures it can boast about, it receives them sure enough (for the civil servants imagine that this is a way of showing their zeal) but later finds itself obliged to correct them. The false figure, a by-product of propaganda, ends up as counter-propaganda.

Even in countries of the free world statistics are sometimes unreliable. If in the United Nations demographic year-book you find the surface of a country given 'at low tide' and not counting 'the surface of frontier waterways', or its population given after the subtraction of 'persons in transit on board ship', you must not allow yourself to be dazzled by these scruples: the figure which follows is still inaccurate. An expert whom I questioned about the population of Ethiopia (from which country he had just returned) told me: 'In theory twenty million. But possibly fifteen or twenty-five.' Even the 'certain' figures lend themselves easily to deceptive extrapolations. In a study by a learned economist I read these lines: 'The techniques of demographic forecasting are among the least uncertain of all. Their hypotheses are based on long-term experience. Starting from a given rhythm of births, their calculations can be made as if on a counting-frame.' This is a good example of the technocratic credulity which in our time has taken the place of simple religious faith. In fact, the graphs in forecasts show a curious tendency to justify the prejudices of the moment. When these have changed other graphs are drawn and other forecasts are made, which in their turn will be proved inaccurate.

The story of the 'forecasts' made in Puerto Rico is enlightening in this respect. Their authors started from the assumption that associated economies must go through similar phases: the Puerto Rican economy would therefore follow, after a certain time-lag, the course of the American economy. Working on this assumption, the demographers considered a strong flow of emigrants towards the mainland to be normal and even supposed that it would increase progressively. They also supposed that the emigrants would come from unproductive sectors and uneducated milieux. On the contrary, the first emigrants to come forward were an élite of skilled workers, and this fact (leading to a new 'colonial' situation) created unexpected emotional reactions in Puerto Rico. Again, the population, better fed than before, was less powerfully attracted by New York. The result was that the emigration figures, which had reached 75,000 men in 1953, dropped to 6,000 in 1960. A surprise which raises doubts about the forecasts made as to the island's birth-rate and the rate of growth of the population.

If migrations, which are carefully counted, are influenced like this by emotional imponderables, what are we to say about data which are not registered at all? It is known that abortion figures are very high everywhere, but it is impossible to give exact estimates. (In France the question was discussed for a long time on the basis of statements made by a solitary midwife in Lyons in 1906!) Some people take these uncertainties as a pretext for ignoring the problem completely. Others draw arbitrary comparisons between abortion and conception. In these delicate matters sample surveys do not have the same value in different countries. Certain British surveys reveal 'reticence percentages' unknown in the United States.

A demographer's library is a huge cemetery of inaccurate forecasts. I have read a certain number of ostensibly scientific works which in the course of the third and fourth decades of this century prophesied an approaching depopulation of Europe. In 1946 a British Royal Commission, appointed to examine the problem of a fall in the birth-rate, found itself faced with a rush of babies. It imagined that this rise was a temporary phenomenon, a mere compensation for the deficit of births during the war, and prudently advised Britain to *maintain* the level of her population. Since then the rise in the birth-rate has continued. The population which was being urged to survive began by increasing by two million inhabitants in ten years (1946 to 1956). Then the rise accelerated. Today we read with amazement this official statement published in May 1950: 'The Foreign Ministers of the United States, the United Kingdom, and France have recognized that the surpluses of population from which several nations in Western Europe are suffering represent one of the most important factors producing stress and instability in the world.' In fact, ten years later Western Europe was going to be *short* of workers.

I am not by any means suggesting that demographers' predictions are of no interest whatever. But modern forecasting must not be regarded as a substitute for astrology. These forecasts, destined in advance to be corrected, are simply working tools. We must not expect statistics to speak an articulate language of which they are quite incapable; we should let them simply bark a few brief warnings. What is most instructive about them is the general direction of their errors.

On this last point one thing is absolutely certain. In our time forecasts of population growth have constantly been *exceeded.* A forecast dating back a few years already seems to belong to another century. The United Nations spend their time correcting their own figures. In 1954 they forecast that in 1980 the world would have a maximum of four milliard inhabitants. In 1958 they expected nearly five milliard for the same date. During the period 1950–60, the increase in population exceeded the predicted level by over 33 per cent in Pakistan and the Philippines, by over 50 per cent in India and Thailand, by over 100 per cent in Southern Korea. In 1954 there was talk of a world surplus of births of thirty million a year; in 1959 the figure was fifty million. In the United States, in January 1962, the census revised its forecast for 1970. Four years earlier it had predicted for that date a maximum population of 202 million inhabitants. This time it raised the figure to 214 million. Twelve million more! The more accurate statistics become, the more clearly they reveal to us positively dizzy phenomena of growth.

This dizziness is a salutary experience. I should therefore like to induce it for a moment in my readers—after which I shall dispense with figures as far as possible. For the space of one page hold on to your chairs. By that I mean cling to your beliefs, to your habits, to your natural optimism, to everything which can prevent you from feeling suddenly uprooted, swept away, annihilated like a straw in a whirlwind. In certain regions of the globe the population increases *four times over* within a single lifetime. Big prolific countries put into circulation in a very brief period quantities of 'souls'—as people used to say—comparable to the total population of a great nation. Between 1940 and 1960 *a whole Great Britain* was added to the United States. If this rhythm is maintained *a China* (of 1950) will be added between 2000 and 2050. In ten years (1931–41) India increased by *a Germany*. This is a crude means of expression but one which has the advantage of showing how long-established countries, burdened with ancient traditions, and profoundly conscious of their unity and value, can be balanced in a few years in the numerical scales of the world by a sudden arrival of babies in some other part of the planet. No doubt, during the same period, these countries themselves have not remained stagnant, but their rate of increase has been lower and has applied to smaller groups. In fifteen years of repopulation France has increased by only half a Tokyo.

In order to imagine the future, let us begin very modestly by considering a single state: Mexico. In 1933 I knew a little country of that name with seventeen million inhabitants. There were thirty-four million in 1960. I therefore write down half a Mexico in my travel memoirs. But this is already untrue. At the *present* rhythm the population doubles in twenty-three years. 'There is no cause for alarm in that,' you may say. 'If the increase in population has been considerable, the increase in production has been even more so.' True. Let us pass over certain recent indications, in the light of which this comparison might have become less favourable. Let us even forget the dark side of the picture: a third of the population illiterate, 800,000 children unable to find room in the schools. And let us go on following the increase. In 2030 (if the rate of growth remains the same) there will be 272 million Mexicans. The present population will be only an eighth of that new Mexico. That state of affairs is not far distant: men alive today will see it. Let us go on. In 2075 there will be over a milliard Mexicans. That milliard will find it difficult to fit inside the country's frontiers. 'In that case,' you will say, 'other countries will accommodate it.' An intellectual, in the calm of his study, can transport at will surplus populations to underpopulated countries. In theory vacant lands in the Sudan and Ethiopia are waiting for India's hungry masses. But the latter would encounter vigorous local resistance if they tried to occupy them. Even if they were admitted to them, the result would be saturation in Africa before long, without any appreciable easing of the problem in India. There have always been financial, political, and social limits to transfers of population. These limits have even become narrower in our time, because the immigration countries have become fiercer in the defence of their standard of living and the emigrants less prepared to put up with the difficult conditions which the pioneers of old used to accept. The great currents which in the nineteenth century or at the beginning of the twentieth century took Italians to America, Indians to Africa, and Japanese to California or Brazil, have disappeared. The remaining currents operate between neighbours, or else inside a political, economic, or ethnical framework (migrations of Irish and West Indians to Britain, Puerto Ricans to the United States, Algerians to France, Jews to Israel). Even within these limits they arouse lively reactions. In 1961 Britain grew tired of receiving every year 70,000 unemployed West Indians whose presence created public disturbances and economic problems. (In London these immigrants, regarded as undesirable neighbours, lowered the value of the buildings where they settled.) The House of Commons passed a Bill allowing the Government to regulate the admission of West Indians 'as required'. This euphemism conceals the resistance of a long-established society to the creation of a foreign proletariat which was difficult to integrate and doubly alien (racially and socially).

However, retaining our optimism, let us ignore these difficulties, assume the world population to be absolutely fluid, and consider, instead of a particular country, the planet as a whole. On this scale the percentage of growth is less striking. At the present rhythm the population will not be doubled for another forty years. But the basic figure is three milliard, which puts an entirely different complexion on the percentage of growth. What is more, the mass is not transportable, except, theoretically, to outer space—but that is just another illusion. Neither the moon, nor Mercury, nor Mars possesses an atmosphere in which men can breathe. Jupiter and Saturn have too much hydrogen and an unbearable gravity. Only the poles of Venus might just possibly take us. But the chief difficulty is that these planets are small, much smaller than the earth, and even supposing that they were habitable, they themselves, at our present rate of growth, would be rapidly saturated. Let us add, to exhaust the subject, that there is no possibility of going outside our planetary system. The stars have temperatures of tens of thousands of degrees and are so far away that men who tried to reach them would die on the way. It would not be they themselves but their skeletons which would be burnt up on arrival. In spite of all the impressive forays we may make into space, we are therefore imprisoned inside a fairly rigid framework and obliged to make the best of it. The obsession with the cosmos which haunts the men of our time is none the less significant. Conscious that they are going to be short of space on this planet, they keep trying to escape. This panic opens no way out, but it constitutes a symptom.

How has this rapid growth come about? The chief explanation is the diminution of mortality. In the past, civilized peoples, arriving among primitive peoples, decimated them in spite of themselves, by bringing them new diseases.

The European soldiers Cortés took to America were already immunized against smallpox. But he also took with him a Negro who was still infectious and who contaminated the Indians. Half of them died and the rest were demoralized. The nineteenth century witnessed another catastrophe: the spread of tuberculosis to the South Sea Islanders. Shivering in the wet clothes which the bigotry of the missionaries imposed on them, they became receptive to the Koch bacillus. Nowadays the supercivilized peoples of the world no longer take illness with them, but health. Since the Second World War, in certain pilot areas (Ceylon, Puerto Rico, etc.) drives against malaria, infantile diarrhoea, and tuberculosis have reduced by half within a few months the deaths caused by these diseases. Extraordinary as these achievements have been, more can be hoped for in the near future. A big American periodical recently launched a campaign for the intensification of the fight against infant mortality. It reminded its readers that every year in the United States 150,000 lives are

QUINTO
BOOKSHOP
48a
Charing Cross Rd.
WC2
Tel: 071-379 7669

06-12-91
17:50
1 077.77

04 •10.00
•10.00CA

06-12-91
17:50
1 07777

04 •1,000
•1,000

lost before or shortly after birth. If the infant mortality rate in America were as low as that in Sweden, 42,000 of them would be saved. This difference between developed countries gives some idea of the room for progress which remains in the underdeveloped countries.

All these deaths which are 'avoided' are, of course, only postponed. In the United States a certain mathematical increase in the overall death-rate (which has remained stable for several decades in spite of the increase in population) is expected as from 2010. But from the demographic point of view this will be a negligible phenomenon. On the basis of the present-day birth-rate and expectation of life, the octogenarians who disappear at that time will have had three healthy children, each of whom will in his turn have had three offspring, who will have themselves reached the procreating age. The dying octogenarians will therefore leave behind them twenty-seven young descendants (who will soon become eighty-one) and their disappearance will be scarcely noticed by the statisticians.

Another factor of overpopulation, particularly noticeable in certain densely populated and economically underdeveloped regions, is the change in manners. Claude Lévi-Strauss, speaking of primitive societies, writes: 'The marriage rules which they apply have a common characteristic: they are designed to limit the fertility rate as far as possible and to keep it constant.' That is a secret which has been lost. We have ceased to observe old customs concerning the minimum age for marriage, the perpetuation of feminine widowhood, the use of one woman by several men, the prolonged interruption of sexual relations after childbirth or during certain sacred periods, which had the effect of delaying, spacing out, or preventing births. While some people are alarmed, for moral or religious reasons, at the progress (small though it is as yet) of birth control, the unprejudiced observer notes a more important phenomenon: the disappearance of its ancient forms.

Six milliard human beings in the year 2000: that, as we have already said, is the figure given by the United Nations three years ago. But it is generally considered that this figure is already out of date and should now be raised. For the movement is accelerating. At the end of the century, so it is thought, the world population will be increasing at such a rate as to double in size in twenty-seven years. Another little effort and our planet will confirm the Malthusian hypothesis by doubling its population in twenty-five years. Let us calculate on that basis. Six milliard (or more) in the year 2000. Twelve milliard in 2025, twenty-four in 2050, ninety-six in 2100. One can already glimpse the Black Friday prophesied by the demographers when each human being will have just one square yard to himself.

You smile, and you are right to smile. You feel sure that before that day comes a brake will have been applied. But what brake? The Marxists think that the victory of their doctrine is written in the future; but they do not regard that as dispensing them from working with all their might to achieve it. We do not show the same fervour in trying to ward off a danger which none the less threatens us all. If we do nothing, 'something' will happen all the same, but that 'something' will be in the nature of a catastrophe. The shortage of space for human parking is, of course, a theoretical limit. The corrective which will come into play beforehand might be of a biological nature. Rats reproduce less in certain conditions of overcrowding. Some American scientists even claim to have detected in them a sort of hormone control of reproduction. Any excessive increase in population, they claim, produces a modification of the pituitary glands which reduces the birth-rate. There is no real point in trying to discover whether this hormone defence mechanism also exists in man, for in him it would eventually be preceded by an intellectual reaction. The first signs of economic asphyxiation would bring home to everyone the dangers of overpopulation and reinforce the usual motives for birth control. Moreover, the distinction here between biology and psychology is not very clear. In their studies on the overcrowding of rats the American biologists speak of *stress*. In modern dictionaries that is an ambiguous word with overtones ranging from shock to fear.

There is another phenomenon which seems to be better substantiated: the reproduction of certain species increases or decreases at the same time as the plants on which those species feed. A large supply of food starts a process of reproduction which accelerates until a famine occurs to restore the balance. This phenomenon can also be observed in the history of mankind. In the course of the last two centuries a dramatic example has been given by a Western European country: Ireland.

In Cromwell's time the natives had been pushed back by the English invaders towards the poor lands in the west. In spite of this unfavourable start, the population suddenly grew in the second half of the eighteenth century. This was the result of the introduction of the potato, a tuber which required little attention, did not mind being left in the ground, and could be shared with the pigs. The Irish, beguiled by these advantages, imagined that their subsistence was assured. They lived in mud huts, with no furniture, windows, or chimneys, and slept on the ground with their animals; but the potato kept them alive. They got into the habit of marrying at an early age. Their women were grandmothers at thirty. The explosion of confidence lasted sixty years, during which time the population trebled.

That Ireland of eight million inhabitants was like a big castle of cards built on fragile economic foundations. In December 1845 it suddenly collapsed: a disease destroyed the whole of the year's potatoes within a few weeks. The following harvests also died, as did most of the cultivators. In the huts groups of people were found dead and alive, equally skeletal, lying on top of one another under blankets. Those who saw these sights were never able to banish them from their memory. First of all an attempt was made to use the unemployed on public works. In 1847 some 800,000 Irish worked on the roads and three million were given help. But England soon found the burden too heavy and suspended the works. Then the starving Irish started leaving the country. In 1848 certain regions in the west were entirely deserted: their inhabitants had moved in hundreds of thousands to Liverpool, Glasgow, or America. Shameless speculators fitted out old boats for them in which they were allowed to crowd together without food. Epidemics decimated them in the course of their long journeys. Out of 89,000 emigrants who set out for Canada, 15,000 never reached their destination. By means of these sacrifices the population of Ireland was reduced to three-quarters of its former strength. The potato, cured of its disease, was able to feed the survivors more or less adequately. The balance had been restored.

Such were the consequences of overpopulation in the Europe of the last century. Fortunately the recurrence of a similar event has become unthinkable in the present-day world. In the face of such suffering no Western government would dare to show the callous indifference displayed at the time by the London government. Moreover, the improvement of communications would enable the agricultural surpluses accumulated by the rich countries to be sent swiftly to the region in danger. But we might have a different sort of disaster, which would not arouse any reactions, for it would not be spectacular. Instead of appearing in the form of piles of corpses, it would be slowly recorded in the statistics of a high mortality rate. In the China of today you cannot see corpses by the roadside as you could in the Ireland of yesterday, but you *can* see queues outside the food shops and children with swollen bellies. Today's victims do not die directly of hunger but indirectly of diseases favoured by undernourishment. The great famines which used to devastate South-East Asia have disappeared. (The last one was twenty years ago, in Bengal.) But a great many human beings are only just above the minimum subsistence level. This multiplication of half-lives is the modern form of the plague. It is difficult to remedy, for only a small fraction (seven per cent) of the world's food enters the world's trade today. On the whole, each great region of the globe feeds itself and thus bears the consequences of the climatic misfortunes which overtake it. The Western surpluses are enough to deal with an emergency situation in a limited zone. They would not be adequate to cope with a world famine.

In point of fact, at the time of writing, the level of nourishment in China is slowly falling. In 1960 the harvest figures were the same as in 1957, which means a drop in the standard of living, since in the interval the population of China has grown by about forty-five million consumers. Some experts go further: they assert that the average harvest of the last three years was only a third bigger than the 1939 harvest, whereas the number of mouths to be fed has increased by nearly a half.

As everybody knows, a penny invested at compound interest at the time of Christ's birth would have become a huge fortune in the course of centuries; but this multiplication did not take place and could not take place. The same will be true of population. But we should like to know when, at what level, and above all by what means, the increase is going to be halted. In this respect the example of Christ's penny is anything but reassuring. Why did it not increase in value in accordance with the theory of compound interest? Because, as Raymond Aron recently reminded us, 'various processes—the devaluation, expropriation, or destruction of material capital or title-deeds—have prevented the excessive growth of invested savings'.

Will the geometrical increase of population be interrupted by similar phenomena: the devaluation or destruction of mankind? The word 'devaluation' has, in this particular case, a precise meaning which we shall define later on. The word 'destruction' must, alas, be taken literally. It means that at a given moment, in spite of all the progress achieved by medical science, the death-rate, after a long period of decline, would rise again.

We must not despair. Mankind—on certain conditions, which we shall mention—does not seem to be incapable of coping with its present task, which is to give adequate nourishment to the three milliard human beings now living on this globe and the other three milliard who are on the way. Ever since Malthus, people have anxiously compared the progress of the world's population with that of the world's food resources. The answer given in the past hundred years has been reassuring. Human ingenuity has discovered new processes which former generations never even imagined. The growth of the species has been accompanied by a growth of Nature. This adjustment has its limits, but they have not been reached yet. It seems that agricultural production per inhabitant has been maintained at roughly the same level as before the war in the world as a whole. The Far East (not including China) has even made rapid progress during the last few years. On the other hand there have been setbacks in Africa, South America, and the Middle East (but in this last region production per inhabitant is still much higher than it was before the war). Moreover, these production figures have to be supplemented by the figures for international aid and trade.

How long can this relative balance be maintained? Each person answers this question according to his temperament or his prejudices. The natalist observes that a planet entirely cultivated in the same way as Holland would support twelve milliard men. The Malthusian replies that the bursting of Holland's frontiers is a more likely event than the 'hollandization' of the globe. The natalist goes on to talk about submarine farms, the cultivation of seaweed, the modification of climates. The Malthusian retorts that we must not expect too much from these expedients; in this respect we may already be on the road of diminishing returns. 'Recent research by English scientists', writes Edouard Bonnefous, 'has shown that the nutritional value of plants treated with artificial fertilizers is perceptibly lower than that of plants fed with organic fertilizers.' According to André Guerrin, there exists a 'rate of capture' for fish and plankton; the return of a fishing-ground which is overexploited diminishes. The debate can go on like this for a long time, with one hypothesis set against another. But in the end the Malthusian wins. However deliriously optimistic his adversary may be, he is always in a position to reply implacably with a date when human multiplication will have exhausted all the resources envisaged. And if he in his turn gives his imagination free rein, that date will indeed seem fairly close. Supposing that all the women in the world decide to procreate at their natural fertility rate, an Illinois professor has calculated that mankind will die of suffocation on 13 November 2026.

The impossibility of indefinite development becomes strikingly apparent if we imagine it as from a date chosen in the past: an American has calculated that 100 people reproducing themselves without restraint during the 5,000 years of world history would have produced two milliard seven hundred million human beings per square foot. Moreover it is just as difficult to imagine an indefinite expansion of *production* at the present rhythm. Overcrowding by goods would precede overcrowding by men. The hundreds of milliards of men and machines which we are asked to imagine by an extrapolation of the present, derive from one and the same fantasy.

In practice, long before famine and overcrowding, tension will occur which will increase the risk of armed conflict. Countries with a rapidly increasing population have a low average age. Their political climate is consequently stormier and their stability lower. Demagogues take it upon themselves to transpose the demographic disease from which they are suffering, to find a scapegoat which will seem to be responsible for it, to eclipse hunger with hatred. (The latter can be aroused in a few hours, whereas it takes several decades to appease the former.) In 1956 Egypt decided to build a new dam at Aswan in the hope of halting, by means of the energy produced, the decline in the standard of living which the country's galloping demography was normally bound to produce. But while unforeseen difficulties were slowing down the work a census revealed two million babies whom the experts had not expected. At one fell swoop the whole undertaking was nullified. To compensate for this setback, Nasser tried to Egyptianize Syria, carried out widespread arrests of 'reactionaries' and subjected a few French diplomats to a pointless trial. The history of this century will be made up of diversions of this sort.

We can already witness a few elementary phenomena of overpopulation. In May 1962 Communist China, like a saucepan filled to the brim, spilled over into Hong Kong. Britain repelled these refugees, Russia failed to invite them into Siberia, while the United States took in a few thousand to ease their conscience. Thus the real attitude of the leading states in the face of demographic expansion is seen to be the same. No birth control on the one hand, no immigration on the other: there is agreement in practice to accept population surpluses and to get rid of them by means of a high death-rate. If the pressure of the birth-rate does not relax, the underdeveloped peoples may come to realize the physical impossibility of improving their lot and become aware of a certain moral strength born of this very despair. This state of mind will become singularly dangerous when a reduction of the cost of nuclear weapons brings them within reach of the poorer states. These weapons are at present the monopoly of fully developed nations (capitalist and Communist) whose relatively high standard of living has made them conservative. When they fall into the hands of desperate peoples who think they have nothing to lose the world will enter the sphere of the unknown.

Must we therefore envisage an exchange of H-bombs which would wipe out half the human race at one blow? From this point of view the last world war was very disappointing. The next one—if it comes—will be less disappointing. Nuclear discoveries may reinvest war with its former regulative function.[2] I refuse, on principle, to envisage this issue, and still more to call it a solution. Besides, there is a less obvious danger which, in fact, strikes me as more menacing: adjustment to overpopulation by recourse to inferior forms of civilization. Instead of three milliard dead men, six milliard living insects. Alas, even this frightful adjustment will not solve the problem. The merit of the extrapolations I have quoted is to remind us that we are imprisoned in a limited space, that is to say in a limited number. We are free to furnish this prison as we please, to occupy it more completely, to pack ourselves into it more tightly, but only up to a certain point. You can fit a dozen people into a small family car by arranging them carefully and by sacrificing their comfort. You cannot fit in thirty. Now there are already five or six of us in this symbolic car and several extra passengers are preparing to get in. Soon we shall have to lock the doors in any case. Ordinary honesty demands that we should warn travellers who have not yet set out.

Two

TWO WORLDS

So far I have spoken of the world's population as if it formed a whole. Progress in communications and demographic awareness tend in fact to unify it. All the same, from now on the problem will have to be broken down. For the population of the globe is divided into a few large masses with quite distinct characteristics.

The areas with a high birth-rate are in Central America, South America, South Asia, and North Africa. The United States and the U.S.S.R. are at a happy mean. Europe is at the bottom of the ladder. The numerical ratio of these masses is changing fairly quickly. Let us suppose that the countries were depicted on the map of the world according to their population. We should see Europe—already such a tiny continent (Paul Valéry called it a 'little cape')—shrink even more, while a huge Asia casts its growing shadow over it. Depending on the region, the same problems arise in such different atmospheres that their data appear to be transformed as a result. The gap between the birth-rates of India and the United States is a narrow one. (Many of my readers will be surprised to learn this.) But the basic conditions, the natural resources, the available capital, the average income, and the openings for employment are so different that this increase is favourable to the United States and disastrous in India.

In the underdeveloped countries a high density of population is nearly always a factor of economic depression. It may seem mathematically beneficial to have a huge mass from which to form an élite. In fact, the contrary is true: quantity tends to exclude quality. Overpopulation increases the relative cost of education. The education of a Brazilian is not as good as that of an English child, but its cost is proportionately twice as great. In the developed countries a similar observation has been made on the family level. On this point the report of the British Royal Commission on Population states: 'Intelligence tests of school-children by different investigators, first carried out in London in 1914 and subsequently in the north of England, Scotland and Bath, the Isle of Wight and other places, all showed that on average the more intelligent children came from smaller families than the unintelligent. Similar studies in America produced the same result.' A later survey in Scotland was also very illuminating. Professor Thomson, the chairman of the committee carrying out the survey, writes: 'The phenomenon of decreasing average score with increasing size of family is fully confirmed beyond all possible doubt.'

Writing this chapter, I have before me three treatises concerning three countries which are very different in situation, climate, living conditions, and political and economic regime: Jugoslavia, Ceylon, and Haiti. These treatises bring out in different but equally convincing ways the disastrous consequences of overpopulation. Defective sowing, the cultivation of unproductive land, rising costs, a drop in the quality of cattle, unemployment, high general and infant mortality, a low standard of education: this is what the Jugoslav treatise notes. The Cingalese report observes that the population pressure in country districts leads to the continual division of property, hence to a retrogression in farming methods, hence to poor harvests, hence to the eventual sale to a richer landowner to whom the peasant had to abandon part of his crops. In Haiti a United Nations mission has noted that the island's farmers, constantly clearing fresh stretches of land to make room for a growing population, have deforested so many steep slopes that the water is now washing the soil down towards the valleys and towards the sea. In this extreme case an increase in population has brought about not just a *relative* dimunition but an *absolute* dimunition of subsistence.

Among the bigger countries there have been two particularly striking examples in recent years of a slowing down of economic expansion due to overpopulation: in India and China. India has had to modify her third five-year plan and abandon certain industrial projects in order to cope with the food requirements of her growing population. China has had to draw on her gold, silver, and currency reserves to pay for cereal imports, and hence give up opportunities to enrich herself by participating in more complex exchanges with the rest of the world. Here again an alimentary deficit has put a brake on industrial development.

One obvious consequence of overpopulation is the growth of unemployment. It is possible to stop recording it, to camouflage it by undertaking useless works, or to share between several individuals tasks which could be performed by one: the essential phenomenon is still there. Time and again, on car journeys in the Far East, I have seen my driver joined by another person who was just as hungry-looking and incompetent. He was there, I was told, to relieve his comrade in case of emergency. Every overpopulated country knows these ghostly doubles who encumber the economy without helping it, and live parasitically on the rations of their 'originals'.

Monsieur Tabah has produced this calculation: in a typical underdeveloped country, with the same birth-rate and death-rate as Algeria, if the national income rose every year by seven per cent (a high figure which could not be reached without considerable foreign aid or despotic government) the consumption per person, in spite of this rise, would be smaller after a quarter of a century if the fertility rate remained the same. The only people who can approve of such a situation are exploiters, both Communist and capitalist. 'We cannot have too many hands', say the rulers of China. That is because they intend to use those hands as tools, without taking into consideration the men to whom they belong. Even from the economic point of view that is a poor system, for in the long run slavery is not very productive. This has frequently been observed in the course of history, and present-day China offers a fresh demonstration of the fact.

Peking's fanatical natalism finds its counterpart in the anxiety of the Japanese employer who is afraid of seeing wages rise as a result of the fall in the birth-rate in Japan (when a rise of that sort is healthy and normal in a country which is in process of developing). These contrary attitudes both belong to what used to be called the 'sweating system'.

The countries of South-East Asia use scarcely more than ten per cent of their national incomes for investment purposes; they have a vast number of illiterates and few skilled workers. If their fertility rate dropped, this would immediately have happy consequences. For fifteen or twenty years the number of producers would stay the same, while the burden imposed by the maintenance of the country's children would be reduced. The standard of food, housing, and education could therefore be raised, and this would lead to an increase in productivity. At the present rhythm, in 1980 there will be only fifty workers in the Malay Federation to provide for 100 children. In Japan (which has just brought its birth-rate under control) at the same date, for the same number of children, there will be 350 adults. Thanks to this favourable situation a decisive step will have been taken: the rapid accumulation of capital will have made possible a rise in the standard of living. A 'pump' will have been set in operation which will start that process of constantly accelerating economic growth of which the West has recently given the example.

In a poor country the number of men can be an advantage only in certain shameful hypotheses. An overpopulated country is like a bear on the stock exchange. He needs a catastrophe in order to benefit from his position. In the event of large-scale nuclear destruction that nation can easily lose part of its population without feeling the pinch. Its overpopulation may even discourage potential aggressors in advance. Rather than add to this saturation, they will turn to countries which still have some land available. From this point of view the overpopulation of India can be represented as an instinctive defence against an eventual invasion by the overpopulated Chinese. Six hundred thousand swarming villages say to the master of Peking: 'You would do better to go and occupy Laos and Thailand: there is still some room left in those countries.' Creating misfortune at home in order to defend oneself against it is a sinister policy. Is it even an effective one? History has often seen—even in our own times—a conqueror expel a native population in order to take its land without caring whether it can find any more.

Let us put ourselves for a moment in that conqueror's place. Is the maximum population from the military point of view likely to be higher than the maximum population from the economic point of view? True, compression provokes expansion. A population surplus is an excellent explosive for starting a war. Before 1940 Germany, Italy, and Japan accumulated babies very much as a terrorist stocks plastic. Perhaps that is what China is doing today. In a local conflict her mass would give her the dual advantage of number and appetite. On the other hand, as a major power, her mass is a weakness rather than a virtue. We have seen that overpopulation is putting a brake on China's industrial development; and nowadays it is industry which is the principal basis of military power. In 1945 Japan had to surrender without having used half her army. Does China's backwardness at least render her less vulnerable than other countries? Perhaps we should turn this proposition round and say that, since her vital points are few in number, only a few well-aimed blows would be needed to destroy the Chinese economy. In Egypt a nuclear bomb on the Aswan dam would reduce the whole country to starvation.

It is often stated that Africa south of the Sahara (except in a few very limited regions, Ruanda Urundi and the north of Nigeria) has no population problem. This statement is doubly deceptive. On the one hand, a country of low density can be overpopulated. 'Empty' Africa has a higher ratio of agricultural population to arable area than Latin America. Arable land remains temporarily useless if it is poor, difficult of access, and short of investment, or if the inhabitants of the region have no technical skill (and overpopulation prolongs this sterility). On the other hand, even where there is no overpopulation, where indeed the term 'underpopulation' would have to be used, the problem arises in a different form. The increase is produced by the surplus of a high birth-rate over a high death-rate: an equilibrium of poverty, combined with a wastage of health and education, which prevents the creation of a reserve. All the economists who have studied these regions are agreed in considering that a rate of increase of population of 1 to 1·5 per 1,000 would be preferable to the present rate of 2 per 1,000 if it were to result from a simultaneous diminution of the birth- and death-rates. The terrible vicious circle would then be broken, by which children 'are born because others have died and die because they have been born'.

For the past hundred years Europe has been limiting her population. This is not the effect of decisions taken by the governments of Europe. The latter, on the whole, have pursued a natalist policy, which did not take into account all the fiscal and social consequences of its principles, but asserted itself by propaganda against and (down to these last few decades) by severe repression of contraception. It is the families themselves which, guided by a sure instinct, have chosen to restrict their numbers, thus saving the continent as a whole from an economic catastrophe.

In France this evolution has often been deplored, for national reasons which were perfectly legitimate but need to be qualified. Leading the way as early as the end of the eighteenth century, France took a risk: that of not being followed straight away by her neighbours. A disparity was, in fact, created between France and Germany which weighed heavily on the relations between those two powers. In the six contingents of recruits (1910–16) who bore the chief burden of the First World War there were twenty-two Germans to ten Frenchmen. This inequality was dangerous, not only because of its material consequences, but also because of the inferiority and superiority complexes which it aroused. However, it tended to bring about a compensatory modification of the diplomatic situation. If the French birth-rate had been higher would Britain have become France's ally? Alfred Sauvy is right in my opinion to ask this question. Albion came to the continent to restore a balance which had been destroyed. If the figures had been the other way round her attitude might also have been the reverse of what it was. Similarly Germany's high birth-rate has not been an unmixed blessing for that state. It inspired her with an imperialist policy which ended up by dividing the country in two, thus bringing the population of free Germany down to the level of the French population (with an identical birth-rate). Germany's adventure can be summed up by saying that she has arrived at a reduction in the birth-rate through overpopulation by way of a tragedy in five acts: war, reparations, unemployment, Hitlerism, partition.

France, it seems, had a choice between two 'histories': one aiming at glory written with a great deal of sperm and blood, the other aiming at happiness by means of a less expensive equilibrium. Each policy was viable, on condition that it remained coherent. Unfortunately France chose a contradictory policy, at once Malthusian and imperialistic, which combined the defects of both concepts. And in the end she managed to avoid a mortal bleeding only by withdrawing from the war for three years (1940–3) in anything but glorious circumstances.

Today France's demographic situation strikes me as satisfactory on the whole. The birth-rate has reached its ceiling at the same level as in 1800, but the real situation is much better than this would suggest. Fewer new-born babies does not necessarily mean fewer young men. On the contrary, the 800,000 annual new-born babies of present-day France will at the age of twenty provide an army of 770,000 adults, whereas the survivors of the new-born babies of the First Empire numbered only 510,000 at the same age. The recent rise in the birth-rate was a welcome phenomenon. It even seems inadequate today, since France is short of labour. But she will soon find herself faced with a rush of young people which may change her point of view.

In any case it is not a bad thing for a country like France to owe some part of her growth to immigration. Welcoming and rearing the sons of overpopulated countries is a duty of human solidarity. From the point of view of 'sacred egoism', it also relieves the nationals of unpleasant work and provides a reserve which makes it possible, in an emergency, to reduce the labour force without putting it out of work. But there is another side to the problem. A long-established country which means to remain 'true to itself' can accept only a limited percentage of immigrants, especially if they are of a very different racial, religious, or social character. By the 1961 Act which we quoted earlier, Britain subtly restricted her West Indian immigration while placing no check on her Irish immigration. Unavowed but excusable racialism. France for her part probably made a mistake, after the Second World War, in rejecting the Italian immigration which was proposed in order to take in Algerian workers who proved more difficult to assimilate.

When, in about 1845, France began to control her birth-rate, she made herself conspicuous in a Europe which continued to pullulate. When, later on, this evolution continued and gathered momentum, it was regarded as a sign of French decadence. It was rather an accurate premonition of the future. As early as the first third of the twentieth century, a falling birth-rate ceased to be an exclusively French phenomenon. On the contrary, while from 1920–4 to 1930–4 the French birth-rate fell only from 20 to 17 per 1,000, the Italian birth-rate—to take only one example—fell from 30 to 24 per 1,000, a fall which was to be accentuated later on. Because France led the way and gradually reduced her birth-rate, the problem of the ageing of her population is less acute than that which faces her neighbour. Her rhythm has now been adopted by most of her neighbours. The birth-rates of Italy, Western Germany, Switzerland, and the United Kingdom stand like that of France between 18·5 and 17·5 per 1,000. These populations are no longer in competition with one another: they are advancing at the same pace. The demographic armistice which has been tacitly concluded between them is one of the firmest foundations of that European unity which is under construction.

As far back as the 1930–5 period the drop in the French

birth-rate slowed down perceptibly. The curve flattened out, giving rise to hopes that it would soon start rising. Was the reason to be seen in the end of the French economic crisis, or the beginning of family allowances? These explanations are partially valid. But the birth-rate curve followed a similar course in the United States, the U.S.S.R., and England. What was happening was therefore a widespread movement, affecting states in different economic and social situations. Was there an instinctive feeling, in those years of tension, of the need to reply to the demographic challenge made by Germany and Japan? (Since overpopulation was invoked by these states as justification for the conquest of 'living-space', the other states had to populate their own space in order to deserve to keep it.) Did a general improvement of the economic situation, due to Roosevelt's New Deal, to the triumph of Keynes's doctrines in Britain, to Hitler's achievement of full employment, and to the Soviet five-year plans, encourage couples to display their confidence in the future by an increase in fertility? (That would not be in the least surprising: the widely held theory according to which a rise in the standard of living encourages birth control is often belied by experience.) Or else, versatility being the characteristic of mankind, did the curves stop falling for the simple reason that they had fallen a long way before? Let us say—because it is the most encouraging formula—that civilized humanity, refusing to commit suicide, took the necessary measures when the time came, to ensure its replacement. But there is always something arbitrary about interpreting in such a rational fashion and from the point of view of society a host of unconcerted individual decisions. When all is said and done, the phenomenon remains somewhat mysterious.

Similarly, the rise in the birth-rate after the war, capable of logical explanation in the belligerent countries by the celebration of delayed marriages and the desire to compensate for war-time losses, spread to the neutral countries where the war had not killed anybody. No doubt the life instinct was stimulated everywhere by a vivid awareness of death. In France the birth-rate rose as the system of family allowances (first under Vichy and then after the Liberation) developed. But it also rose in Britain and the United States, where there were at that time no such allowances. It is true that in these two countries other measures may have had the same effect. In Puerto Rico I was told that one of the causes of the boom in births after the war was the granting of pensions to the wives of men who were called up; these women found themselves supplied with an income which they had never had at their disposal before. In Britain, during the war, *per capitem* rationing was an indirect family grant. The prices of food and clothing were fixed by controls and subsidies, while incomes rose. Because of shortages, everybody was badly off, but, in contrast with pre-war times, large families were not worse off than the rest.

Between the French 'falling out of step' in 1845 and the general alignment of 1945 exactly a hundred years had passed. In the meantime Europe had unloaded part of her surplus on the other side of the Mediterranean, something which after a few decades produced the return shock of the wars of colonial liberation. In North Africa the process has had some curious consequences. Frenchmen, Spaniards, and Italians, forming a surplus in their own countries, crossed the Mediterranean and propagated technique and hygiene on the far shore. The result was a considerable increase in the Moslem population, which now takes this as a pretext for expelling the Europeans in the name of the majority principle, another 'colonial' contribution. We could philosophize at length on this subject; instead, let us examine the near future.

In the countries of Western Europe as a whole, the number of consumers is going to increase by twenty-eight million between 1960 and 1970. The workers will increase less than the two inactive groups (the young and the old). To balance this increased burden, an annual growth of national productivity of one per cent will be necessary. It is only after that point that an improvement in the standard of living can begin. To overcome this handicap we shall have to organize our production better, while guiding the young and watching the old so that they do not overtax the growing resources which will have to be placed at their disposal. The effort will not be unduly arduous. In order to 'stay where we are' we shall only have to go at a trot, while others will be obliged to gallop; and minor difficulties are more stimulating than depressing. If it were not for this moderate growth we might feel a sort of panic with regard to the countries with a rapidly growing population.

Even so, Europe's proportion of the world population is going to shrink. According to the United Nations experts, it will fall before the end of the century from 23 per cent to 15 per cent, while North America will drop only from 6·7 per cent to 5 per cent and Asia will rise from 55 per cent to 60 per cent. We must not let this alarm us unduly. It means only that the Europeans are going to resume the same proportional position that they occupied three centuries ago. Besides, as we have seen, numbers are not power. Our moderate growth will maintain our dynamism without exposing us to dangerous adventures. We shall probably even have occasion to consider with a certain pity the ups and downs of less prudent peoples. Good luck, young old Europe!

To study the *overpopulation of the developed countries* we must turn rather to the United States, where we find a combination of a higher birth-rate (24 per 1,000 as against 18 per 1,000) and a superior industrial power. Signs are appearing of a risk of overcrowding. 'Between the Chinese rhythm and the American rhythm', writes Jean Fourastie, 'the time gap in producing a density of 10^3 is only forty-five years.' But in the near future the problem is not one of overpopulation with regard to material resources, but with regard to the demands of human dignity. The danger is not hunger but the degradation of civilization.

The considerable increase in the population of the United States since the Second World War has become localized, in practice, in the large cities, which themselves have been tending to merge into one another. Jean Gottmann, in an interesting study, has given the name *Megalopolis* to the almost uninterrupted urban mass which stretches from Boston to Washington, grouping together thirty-seven million inhabitants. This will soon be balanced by a western Megalopolis in California, from San Diego to Santa Barbara. These huge agglomerations, attractive though they are in many respects, also have something infernal about them. Engines fill them with noxious fumes. Just as sunbathing was becoming fashionable among their inhabitants, they were cut off from the sun by an industrial fog, pierced here and there by skyscrapers like cries for oxygen and light. Every day the factories seem to start up just in time to intercept the ultra-violet rays. Plants suffocate, while men and houses have to defend themselves continuously against dirt by washing and painting. Around these urban monsters, car accidents wreak havoc comparable to that made by war. (I have read that between January 1940 and June 1941 Britain had 41,000 people killed by the war and the United States had 51,000 people killed on the roads.)

To house their growing families, the city dwellers move out into the suburbs, hoping to find fresh air and cheap living there. But this movement soon results in the urbanization of the surrounding countryside. The proportion of concrete and stone (buildings, roads, car parks, etc.) constantly increases at the expense of the earth which the city dweller left his city to find. The trouble is that he brings with him the overcrowding from which he would like to escape. He arrives not only with his children, but also with his cars, which likewise need sleeping space. The second child has competed, in the family budget, with the second car. The third child, on the other hand, arriving in a scattered town and an increased budget, makes that second car necessary. This is excellent for big business. But in proportion as the number of cars increases, the services they obtain diminish. At certain times of the day they move through the big cities more slowly than a horse in 1900. Even outside, they are overtaken, slowed down, tamed by the huge weekend traffic. Processions form up which, every now and then, all together, take a jump forward. The wheels turn on white or yellow lines, as if they were caught by rails. The driver who tries to go out into the open country comes home hemmed in like the bull which is brought back to the pen by oxen at the end of a Portuguese bullfight. The car, once an instrument of escape, is now just a means of travelling to a more efficient instrument of escape: the boat. But overcrowding is beginning to spread to the waterways too.

In New York fresh immigrants come flocking in, Negroes or Puerto Ricans, whose arrival puts the natives to flight. The latter resign themselves during the day to mixing with the intruders in the old city, but in the evening they move out to satellite towns comparable to exclusive clubs, to which only people of their colour and standing are admitted, and on Sundays they shut themselves up in their collective parks. (This movement of repulsion is backed up by a few objective reasons, for 'coloured' immigration produces a fall in the standard of education and an increase in delinquency.) On both sides of the fence taxation rises: in the old districts because the rich taxpayers have moved out, in the new districts because services have to be created there for them.

Have the fugitives at least found happiness in their suburbia? No. Jane Jacobs has given a fascinating description of the neurasthenia which lays hold of them in that fake countryside where the 'green spaces' consist of a few poor strips of turf. That varied, nourishing sociability, that warm awareness of belonging to a community which the Americans call 'togetherness', has disappeared. People talk nostalgically of the cramped towns of old, where the houses dated from several periods, and the children were safe in the streets because the neighbours always kept an eye on them. Those neighbours are now strangers. Nobody goes for a walk any more. If the police catch sight of a pedestrian they will warn him of the risks he is taking by walking alone across vast spaces which are at once urbanized and unsupervised. Behaving 'normally' means sitting snugly in your little individual fortress: house or car. You no longer go to the cinema, but sit in front of your television set—the only easy outlet—and travel round the world in pictures when the news bulletins are shown (a news item, an advertisement; an advertisement, a news item). There are no workmen in the neighbourhood, so you must do your own painting and repairs. And when you have spent a few years living like this, driving for two hours every day, browsing on concrete and plying every conceivable trade, there is only one thing that you would like to do: go and rest in a real town. A movement in the opposite direction is beginning. After raising their children in the suburbs couples are going back to the centre to spend their old age there.

While the cities are being devitalized by extension, the villages are shrinking to death. Many are now nothing but a string of houses along a main road. Nobody can live in them unless he has a car. George Kennan concludes the description he gives of one of them with this confession of failure: 'We have unthinkingly allowed the internal combustion engine to change our lives.'

Last winter in Washington I listened to a conversation between an optimist and a pessimist.

'Our Megalopoles,' said the former, 'can't be as unpleasant as they say, because people go on crowding into them. Seventy per cent of the population of the United States are now urbanized. And yet we don't have to worry about running short of space, because our towns cover only one per cent of the territory. The air pollution is unpleasant, but on the east coast the Atlantic winds purify the atmosphere. What's more, a system of filters is being brought to perfection. By the year 2000 the danger will have been overcome. A lot of water has been wasted? Well, we'll ration it, that's all, and later on we'll distil sea-water. In the United States of the twenty-first century proteins will be provided by mushrooms. We'll grow giant vegetables. A single potato will be enough to feed four people. In winter we'll wear thermic clothes. The ice regions will be made habitable, or, better still, they will be thawed out. Heating up the Bering Strait will cause fog in Naples? That's the Neapolitans' look-out!'

'You say,' retorted the pessimist, 'that people are falling over themselves to come and live in our big cities? That doesn't mean that they like it there. Indeed, it is probably the distinctive characteristic of our urban civilization that a great many people are irresistibly attracted to it without finding satisfaction in it. They feel very much as we do when, soaked with bright colours by second-rate painters, we go back to the old masters. We know that they are better painters, but in contrast they strike us as dull, grey, boring. They have been spoilt, not replaced. If the inhabitants of New York were really satisfied with their life you wouldn't have half of them under treatment for nervous diseases. The space you talk about is theoretical. Nobody is going to go and live in the deserted farmhouses; on the contrary, more of them are going to be abandoned. We shall go on living in an ever-increasing dual congestion: that of the towns in winter, and that of the seaside and the parks in summer. Our thirst will be quenched. But what sort of water shall we be given? The New York water, which tastes of the chemical used to disinfect it, is already undrinkable. We shall give barely adequate food to more and more people, and make them live in less and less pleasant places. What an achievement! Admittedly we have prolonged human life, but what do we do with the extra time? The years we have added to the end of life are scarcely worth living. The hours we have gained through technical progress are lost again in traffic jams and administrative formalities. Being jolted along in vehicles for two hours a day from the suburbs to the city, from the city to the suburbs, along the same monotonous road, without really being able to think, read, or do anything—is that really living?'

I had arrived late for my appointment with the optimist and the pessimist, having spent a good quarter of an hour making my way through my hotel, which was crowded with a 'convention'. From my room to the reception desk there were fifteen floors. At each floor the huge lift stopped to engulf members of the convention, who, anxious to maintain some semblance of personality, sported their names on badges. After that I had had to elbow my way across the entrance hall, just as in an underground station during the rush hour. This physical experience of overcrowding inclined me to agree with the pessimist. On reflection, however, it struck me that the optimist was justified in counting on human ingenuity to find in the near future the material solution to the problems created by the increase of population. The discoveries which he prophesied may not come, but others will be made which nobody has thought of yet. Only a few years ago some neo-Malthusian authors announced that American consumption would soon exhaust all the world's raw materials. Those forecasts of theirs already make us smile. Let us beware of making ourselves look equally ridiculous with more gloomy predictions. In any case, the pessimist did not so much deny possibilities as express dislikes.

His point of view, which some people will contemptuously describe as 'aesthetic', strikes me as none the less worthy of consideration. For we must not only ask ourselves whether means of adjustment will be found, but also whether those means of adjustment will be progressive or regressive from the point of view of civilization. What seems certain is that they will have to be frequently revised. Each solution that is found will create new problems. The disappointments of suburbia will be followed by other disappointments. Already, at the present time, a quarter of the American population moves house every year. This movement will gather speed. To keep up with the combined force of numbers and technical progress, the American will have to drive himself harder and harder, call on all his resources under the pretext of relaxing, and travel far and wide in search of a tranquillity which will disappear on the way. A terrifying process, for it contains within it an unconscious appeal for a catastrophe capable of stopping it.

I have been talking about American cities. I could have taken a more dramatic example: the Tokyo of ten million inhabitants which Robert Guillain has recently described. A city which holds the world record for accidents (60,000 victims in 1960). A city of single-storeyed wooden houses, built in the expectation of a future earthquake, resigned in advance to disappearing. A city without landmarks, 'an endless agglomeration of large villages'. A city without sewers, without gutters, without pavements, without street-lighting, crossed by trains and cars which cut across one another without benefit of gates, and where 'on the underground platforms, during the rush hour, there are battalions of employees whose sole duty is to push from behind the passengers trying to board the trains or to extract those wishing to get out by pulling at their clothes'. I could also have described Canton and Shanghai, which I visited not long ago: shapeless, soulless cities, peopled with blue ants, crisscrossed by human-drawn vehicles, lit by pale electric light. I could have referred to Calcutta, 'the capital of overpopulation', whose pavements are covered at night with recumbent bodies, and where the struggle for living-space is fought, not, as in the American suburbs, between roads and parks, but between 'hen-coops' and humble market gardens. These cities are far away and most of my readers will never see them. Yet we belong to a single world which is shrinking all the time. The cancers developing out there might well reach us one day and proliferate on our soil.

I talked about the United States because that country serves as a model for the rest of the world. If the Far East succeeds in extricating itself from chaos its cities will begin to resemble American cities. The attempts being made by the Americans to dominate their urban monsters are consequently of interest to all mankind. Theoretically, the best solution would be to raze the existing cities to the ground in order to build others better suited (temporarily) to the economic and demographic conditions of our time. This would be terribly inconvenient. It would also be impossible, because what has been built has to be paid for first. For this reason a British scientist who recently published his predictions for the next quarter of a century forecast that men would reach the moon, but that our cities would change only very slightly.

In order to solve the traffic problems of the near future the authorities will doubtless have to limit the use of private cars, those vehicles which take so much room to move so few people. More widespread use of public transport will slow down the growing encroachment of machines on living-space. (It has already been decided to build a railway across Los Angeles, from Beverly Hills to El Monte, to serve the Californian Megalopolis.) Similarly, in order to facilitate the rationalization of living conditions, the powers-that-be may come to prohibit any sort of social or racial segregation, and enforce a proximity which will end up by producing a certain cross-breeding.

There are always solutions, but they are more or less satisfactory. In fact we shall have to choose between increasingly severe disadvantages. Whoever wants to breathe will have to wait. Whoever wants to travel quickly will have to abandon the idea of travelling alone. Whoever wants to limit the dangers of road travel will have to be canalized. Other adjustments will follow which we cannot even imagine. Each will involve the loss of a little freedom or comfort. A certain amount of space is essential to human dignity. The inhabitants of the Megalopoles of the future will no longer have that space at their disposal. Whether overcrowding is vertical or horizontal makes no difference to this fundamental degradation. Sensibility dies even faster in the 'radiant cities'.

For the past century, first by means of immigration, then by means of a high birth-rate, numbers, which made it possible to pay for machines within a record time, have been the driving force of the American economy. That great, empty virgin country, with its huge resources, was able to absorb and multiply the surplus population of Europe. Now, although the flood shows no signs of slowing down, a certain saturation is becoming apparent. The first reaction of the American producer is to play his cards more energetically than ever. Advertising is now addressed chiefly to the young. It catches them at the age when, without thinking very much about it, people form habits. Tobacco is a cause of cancer? This discovery, which impresses adults, has less effect on adolescents. So an attempt is made to start them smoking early in life, in the hope that later they will be unable to stop. The teenagers of America are already the debtors of big business, and will pay their debts only to contract new ones. (In fact they will spend the whole of their lives redeeming their debts.) As for the children, it is not even necessary to indoctrinate them: they behave instinctively just as the producers would wish. Mussolini once observed, in support of his natalist propaganda: 'The child is a remarkable consumer, for he destroys everything: his books, his toys, his clothes.' In Connecticut the little vandal spends thirty-six dollars a year on toys. It is scarcely surprising that he should be popular with the business men of his country. How, in the end, are we to explain the American 'baby boom'? Are those sweet children the progeny of their fathers and mothers, or of General Electric and General Motors?

Today, however, unemployment is growing. Eighty million people are going to be added to the population of the United States in the next twenty years. Now, according to an investigation carried out by a group of experts from an American university, the country's consumer requirements can be met during that period without any increase in the number of producers. Automation is going to put out of work, not only factory workers, as is often believed, but also white-collar workers. Up to now, workers expelled from the primary and secondary sectors of the economy found it easy to obtain work in the tertiary sector (services). Today the machine follows hard on their heels in that sector. The firm of Macy's has just finished testing its first 'electronic vendor'. This machine can sell thirty-six different products in various quantities, take money, give change (and even reject bad coins). What is going to become of the shop assistant in flesh and blood? It is not her humanity that is going to save her: with her stereotyped smile and her automatic thank you, she is already nothing but a less efficient machine.

Although six per cent of the workers of America were unemployed, and although the increase in population should normally put at least a million men a year on the labour market, the total number of applications for employment in December 1961 was the same as in December 1960. Discouraged by the unfavourable opportunities available to them, hundreds of thousands of Americans had preferred to stay at home and live on their relatives. It is much too soon to draw any conclusions from this phenomenon. Probably most of these abstentions were cases of premature retirement. If tomorrow it was the adolescents who could not find any openings the number of juvenile delinquents would increase still further. One remedy would be to keep them at school, to give them more extensive professional training. But with what object in view? Following the recent line of development, one is led to predict that in 1970 over a third of the total labour force will consist of women. Will some of them have to be sent home? In that case it would be advisable to train them for leisure, for in their homes, too, machines are taking their places.

Georges Friedmann has described the breaking up of human labour into fragmentary tasks and the frustration which is the result. Nowadays a great many workers hanker after a state of stupefaction. Pending the arrival of that total automatization which will completely abolish the personal participation of man in production, they would like to live to the sound of music, with earphones clipped to their heads, while an *inner worker* went through the motions of their work for them. They are even opposed to any attempt to make their work more interesting, for that would force them to be intellectually present. They prefer a 'medullary' job which allows them to dream the day away. The development of automation is going to create a new class division. On the one hand, a small aristocracy, capable of close communication with the machines and alone allowed to put questions to them. On the other hand, a proletariat with no hope of emancipation and whose vital interests will lie entirely outside its work. But the super-industrial civilization will pursue it from the workshops in which it daydreams to the home where it hopes to live. It is already mechanizing its pleasures.

Thus a secret, gnawing boredom is born, the boredom of the man who no longer feels in close contact with his own life. It is hard to trace the progress of the disease, because the means of escape are constantly increasing in number. But they provide no real remedy: one can be bored in the midst of pleasurable distractions.

. . . . .

The big cities of Europe also have traffic problems, an increasing number of heart attacks and neuroses, and juvenile delinquents, and soon they are going to find themselves subjected to atomic blackmail. All of them are approaching bursting-point. Attempts will be made to push it away by staggering working-hours (at the risk of upsetting marriages and friendships), by prohibiting individual transport and lodgings, by moving cemeteries outside, by limiting the number of stadiums, by expelling newcomers, and by peopling satellite towns sprung straight from the planners' brains and which will scarcely have time to be humanized before they in their turn are overcrowded.

Paris absorbs the whole of the increase in the French population. To relieve her of her present congestion, people have suggested expelling government and parliament, separating the newspapers from their printing works, and sending the university into the country. Paris would thus lose what gives her her intellectual vivacity, her influence, her *tempo*. She is being asked in fact: 'What do you prefer? Overcrowding or dispersal? Suffocation or the loss of your soul?' In order to avoid the choice, people are gathering at the gates of the city. In their flats with paper-thin walls, the inhabitants of the big apartment houses share willy-nilly their neighbours' lives, without experiencing any more either friendly sociability or real isolation. The French are also in danger of running short of water—less than the Americans, but that is because they do not wash much. (Ten million country people—over a fifth of the total population—are still waiting for running water, and the national figure for bathrooms is very low.) According to a statement by the Prefect of the Seine, if a serious fire broke out, or if the Parisians failed to go on holiday, there would be no water in Paris in summer above the third floor. Lastly, the fish are disappearing from the polluted rivers of France and the underground waterways are threatened by poisonous infiltrations.

In certain big cities in Europe and America a halt in the fall of the death-rate has recently been noted. It has been explained by pollution of the atmosphere and the increase in traffic or nervous accidents due to the tensions of city life. It is too early to judge. In any case a higher mortality would not relieve the congestion in the big cities, for immigration constantly provides them with far more inhabitants than their poisons can eliminate. Even if more people die there in the future, this influx will not slow down as a result. It may soon resemble a rush of moths coming to burn themselves in the flame of a torch.

Taking into account the rural exodus, France will have to create three million jobs before 1975. That will not be possible without more planning and an increase in social mobility. I spoke earlier of stimulating difficulties. But there are drugs whose effects, stimulating at first, becomes depressive if they are used to excess. A Frenchman to whom the State dictated in advance, in the public interest, the trade he had to choose and the town where he had to live, would feel that he had lost part of his freedom.

Other European countries are more seriously threatened. Britain can no longer feed its growing population cheaply, as it has been able to till now. Within the foreseeable future, Holland is going to feel a shortage of space. (She reclaims land from the sea, but that process cannot profitably be carried out indefinitely.) The widening of economic frontiers and the mixing of populations will make it possible to deal with these problems. They cannot simply be ignored. We also have to face up to a world-wide phenomenon unprecedented in human history. Only yesterday there was no sign of it. Nations were concerned only about partial competition between neighbours. The gap between the populations of France and Germany was enough to occupy the thoughts of Frenchmen and Germans. Today the horizon is widening. The United States feel no gratitude towards Hitler for having presented them with a start of thirty million men over the U.S.S.R.; they are not even aware of it. This is because the developed countries are beginning to feel a certain solidarity in the face of a menace which is threatening them all: the 'demographic aggression' of the underdeveloped countries. We should not be afraid of using this expression, for it was a citizen of an overpopulated country, hence a country guilty of this involuntary aggression (India), who coined it. The moderation we have managed to observe entitles us to raise our voice and invite the other nations to join in the common fight against this scourge.

The effects of a rapid increase in population are comparable to those of a sudden flood of refugees produced by an invasion or a natural calamity. It is impossible to ensure the survival of all while respecting the freedom of each. As a result of practical considerations, the place of work is becoming to an increasing extent the centre of human life. People eat there, vote there, think there (through propaganda). The family is on the down grade and the individual is considered as a 'case' who needs to be socialized to be cured. In a society in process of being organized, overpopulation almost automatically leads to collectivism. This is perhaps the explanation of Mao's return to a natalist policy in 1957. Communist China is forcing herself to apply his doctrine by invading herself. An army of babies is the instrument of her revolution—a new-born child is a unique creature, a contrivance which has never been tried before: this is the element of the unknown which appeals to the parents. But these differences, when multiplied, lead, paradoxically, to uniformity.

I spoke earlier of insects. The word has not simply a pejorative meaning. Indeed we must admire the organizing ability of the ant, the bee, and the termite. 'The ant', writes Michelet, 'is openly and fervently republican.' But is the ant's republic the one we want? In it, instead of free co-operation, there is established an automatic co-ordination between indistinguishable individuals, passively reacting to certain 'stimuli'. The human race too is capable of practising (though so far less perfectly) this sort of solidarity. But it is endowed with a differential element, generally called 'psychological', whose scope modern science has limited without succeeding in eliminating it. From this element we derive our pride in our humanity, and it is important to find out whether the pressure of numbers is going to lead us to get rid of it as a useless accessory, as an obstacle to a collective achievement which we would agree to regard as superior to our own development.

The curse of a 'perfect' organization is that it functions just as well (or even better) in a world devoid of all meaning. J. H. Fabre succeeded in making some processionary caterpillars go round in a circle for a week by placing the first caterpillar behind the last. It is frightening to read about this experiment. Are not we ourselves already close to repeating it? Mankind in the second half of the twentieth century is made up of two groups of ants—one group following the American ant, the other group following the Soviet ant—which will soon be going round in a vicious circle, since the Soviet ant has started following the American ant (unless the reverse is the case). One of these days we might find ourselves engaged despite ourselves in that terrifying 'metamorphosis' which Kafka has described. His story tells of the transformation of a man into a centipede. At first the change is almost imperceptible: the man feels nothing but a slight stiffness in his hindquarters. But in the end the ex-man finds himself equipped with a considerable number of little waving legs which go in the direction they decide without consulting him. This theme must be characteristic of our times, since Ionesco has treated it again in *Rhinoceros*. This time the change is into a horned animal. But the metaphor does not matter. Let us simply note this fact: our poets, our visionaries, are haunted by the fear of a regressive evolution of mankind.

I can easily imagine a reader of the year 2000 exhuming my book and saying: 'This is funny! The author thought we were going to turn into insects!' Once he had been transformed, and also adjusted to this transformation, man would cease to be aware of it. Or else he would consider himself superior, on account of his better social organization, and be surprised to find his rise regarded as a fall. 'There', you may say, 'there is an irreducible difference of viewpoints. But it is the viewpoint of the man in question which matters. A slave who enjoys his slavery is not a slave.' To accept this argument, one would have to be convinced first of all that the human insect will complete his 'metamorphosis'. I refuse to believe that he will. He will struggle free at the last moment, like a man on the point of being caught by the frost.

In the end we shall see the triumph of that explosive force which we call human liberty. My only fear is that the reaction will be delayed too long, and thus be terribly painful.

If we should fail to react in time we might perhaps see the fulfilment of the prophecy made in 1962 by Donald Michael in a study written for the American Centre of Democratic Studies: 'Frustration and the feeling of the uselessness of life might, when the time came, produce a war of despair, ostensibly directed against an outside enemy, but whose aim would really be to humanize society by destroying its technological basis.'

Three

THE INVESTORS IN MEN

THE problems of population have become increasingly acute in our time. But they have always existed and have been treated in different ways by two schools of thought.

Aristotle in his day was the leader of one of those schools. He said: 'Ten men do not make a city, but nor do ten times ten thousand men.' If, he explained, there are too few men in a political unit, they risk losing their independence, and, if there are too many, their freedom. But it was the second danger which he most dreaded. If he were to come back among us today the sight of China would confirm him in his fears. Plato recommended a combination of measures, some restrictive, others natalistic. Among the former were late marriage, abortion, and a halt to procreation after a given number of years of married life. (An age-gap of twenty years between husband and wife would make it possible to synchronize the cessation of sexual activity.) Among the latter was the creation of a corps of 'nuptial inspectors' whose task would be to fight against depopulation. In the eighteenth century the natalist Rousseau and the 'eugenist' Condorcet continued the debate. In the twentieth century Henri Bergson declares: 'If you let Venus work her will she will bring you Mars.' Unfortunately, the contrary is not true: Mars is no longer capable of ridding us of Venus's surplus children. So Gaston Bouthol proposes 'finding a substitute for him'. Two names dominate the whole discussion: those of Malthus and Marx. The former because he was obsessed by the danger of overpopulation. The latter because he completely ignored it, an attitude which has also had far-reaching consequences.

Everybody knows the Malthusian Law, by which subsistence can increase only in an arithmetical ratio (3–6–9–12), whereas population normally increases in a geometrical ratio (3–6–12–24). This law is incorrect. A great many writers have taken pains to prove this, and it is this attempt at refutation which has made Malthus famous. The effort, however, was useless, for Malthus himself, towards the end of his life, had abandoned his 'laws'. He admitted that certain parts of the world were capable of supporting a considerable increase in population in the course of the next few centuries. However, fortunately for him, nobody noticed this correction which, putting an end to the controversy, could have consigned him to oblivion. Similarly there has been a great deal of comment on Toynbee's theory according to which history is a collection of forty civilizations which have followed an identical pattern of development; but scarcely any attention has been paid to the later writings in which he admitted that those civilizations none the less differed considerably from one another. It is by exaggerating a sound thesis that a man obtains fame. If Freud had not reduced infantile sexuality to a few patterns he would have remained an unknown psychiatrist. It has since been shown that those patterns oversimplified the facts, but in the process Freud's name was made famous. The same thing happened with Malthus. One mystery remains: did the inventors themselves believe in their 'laws', or were those dogmatic formulas never anything more than publicity?

During Malthus's own lifetime the chief reproaches levelled at him were of a moral nature. His crime was to have stated that throughout the whole history of mankind sexual desire remained constant. To say that to respectable British citizens, in the Pre-Romantic period when tuberculosis was considered a sign of spirituality, was an unforgivable insult. The Puritans felt themselves reduced to the level of wild animals. Poor Malthus! He was accused of obscenity. Right-minded people refused to shake hands with him. Yet he accepted no other form of birth control but chastity. He has been credited just as gratuitously with a reactionary attitude in economic and social matters. Yet he had stated as one of his principal aims 'the reduction of mortality among the poor.' In reply to Adam Smith, who had called upon the poor to make sacrifices in the interests of economy, Malthus had written: 'The principles of saving, pushed to excess, would destroy the motive to production. If every person were satisfied with the simplest food, the poorest clothing, and the meanest houses, it is certain that no other sort of food, clothing, and lodging would be in existence'. A century later Keynes was to quote this text to the conservatives of his time.

True, if Malthus returned to this world he would have some considerable surprises. He would find that the great wars of recent times have not interfered with demographic expansion. In the past, armed conflicts occurred periodically to mop up population surpluses. That seemed necessary and even desirable. 'If there isn't a war, we'll have to go about like gypsies,' said a sixteenth-century peasant whose remark has come down to us. Montaigne was expressing a widely held opinion when he spoke of war as a 'bleeding'. But nowadays that remedy seems as out-of-date as the bleedings practised by the doctors of his day. In our times penicillin alone has been sufficient to compensate for the slaughter carried out by the tanks and planes. The world population even took a decisive leap forward after the massacre of 1939–45. In 1950–1 the Korean War killed a million men, which is not an insignificant number; but in the course of that same year ten million little Chinese were born. True, at the same time and in the same part of the world there were executions of 'enemies of the people' for various crimes (official Chinese figure: two and a half million; private estimates: between three and twenty million); and in 1950–3 there was a 'campaign against corruption and sabotage' which was as deadly as the persecution of the Kulaks in Russia in 1930. (Mention might also be made, for the record, of a wave of suicides at the end of the period of the

'Hundred Flowers'.) These are trifling details. 'One Paris night will make good all that,' said Napoleon on the evening after a battle. 'Peking nights' have long ago 'made good' the Korean War and the Red Terror. A nuclear cataclysm might be able to cope with this overpopulation. But already there has been a proposal to nullify its effects by founding a 'sperm bank'. Once this bank had been created, the begetters could disappear without harming their progeny. Their substitutes would be ready in advance. When the time came they would only have to be 'unfrozen' as required.

This dual failure (of chastity and war) would disconcert Malthus. On the other hand, he would be less surprised than has been suggested to learn that the European population has grown considerably during the past hundred years, and that its average income, its consumption, and its education have none the less developed enormously. He would even observe that this splendid development has been able to occur only because the European population has followed his advice. During the century following his death demographic expansion was accompanied and finally slowed down by a decrease in the birth-rate. The birth-rate started falling in Sweden in 1830, in France in 1845, in England in 1870. Those who denounced Malthus in public followed his doctrine in private.[4] In so far as the multiplication of the species is concerned, his theory has now been confirmed, and in some cases surpassed, in certain parts of the world. For he forecast an increase in a geometrical ratio only among unchecked populations. But today that type of increase may be seen even in countries which have declared themselves in favour of birth control and are beginning to practise it (for example in Pakistan).

What would undoubtedly grieve him most is the fact that the instrument of 'checking' has been contraception and not continence. He would indeed be positively horrified to learn that such behaviour is called 'Malthusian'. And if he were told that some high ecclesiastical authorities now sometimes regard recourse to these practices as a moral duty he would lose all hope in the salvation of the Protestants. In the twentieth century he would not have recognized himself entirely in anyone but Gandhi. The latter, in a conversation with Margaret Sanger, the birth-control propagandist, admitted that a couple could make do with three or four children, but promptly added that in that case they ought to confine themselves to having intercourse on three or four occasions. The rest of the time the wife should repulse her husband and if necessary leave him. Gandhi in his early youth had not by any means observed this strict morality. He even states in his autobiography that he would have died of exhaustion if he had not been parted from his wife. But later he had come to loathe this 'degradation'. It would be hard to find a better example of the secret bond which often links strictness and weakness.

Marx instinctively ignored anything which might draw attention away from his principal subject: the rule of property.[5] But attempts have been made since his death to use his doctrine to give an ostensibly scientific backing to natalism. According to Marx, when all the elements which go to the composition of an object have been removed there remains a net product which is the increase in value produced by *labour*. If one accepts that labour is *always* productive of wealth, then one must regard any increase in population as beneficial. The Chinese Communists have been particularly ardent in their support of this interpretation since the failure of their attempt at birth control.

In 1956 Peking had launched a huge propaganda campaign in favour of birth control, with an official speech by Chou En Lai. In March 1958 the Minister of Public Health could still declare to Tibor Mende: 'If the increase in our population does not keep level with a planned birth-rate, the resulting disparity will prevent the country from emerging rapidly from poverty and becoming strong and prosperous.' The following year the campaign was abandoned. It was even maintained that it had never taken place. Why? I tried to find an answer to this question on the spot. It seemed to me that several explanations could be credited simultaneously.

The Chinese government came up against practical difficulties (largely due to the lack of medical personnel) which prevented it from carrying out its birth control policy. According to the official Chinese statistics, the annual increase in the population, stabilized at thirteen million between 1953 and 1956, leapt to twenty-one million in 1957 and twenty-three million in 1958. That was the result of two years of birth 'control'! In March 1959, at Shanghai, I asked what the city's birth-rate had been the previous year. The answer was: 36 per 1,000 (as compared with 24 per 1,000 in 1950). This figure for a big city suggests even higher rates in country districts, probably close to the records for America (Guatemala: 49 per 1,000) and for Africa (Guinea: 62 per 1,000). The Shanghai doctor who gave me the figure had begun by saying: 'My impression is that the birth-rate has gone down.' That may, indeed, have been the impression he had gained around him, in the restricted environment of his hospital. On the urban scale, and even more on the national scale, the illusion was dispelled. Continuation of the experiment was therefore postponed to a later date, in the hope that the progress of education in the meantime would allow it to be resumed with greater hope of success.

Mao Tse Tung then hit upon the idea of using for public works the human material which the high Chinese birth-rate offered him. Within the context of this policy, there could not be too many births. The discovery came just in time to cover and magnify the failure of the birth-control policy. National pride may also have played its part: China herself hopes to invent a new contraceptive technique.[6] Finally, as we have seen, over-population brings in its train certain forms of collectivism, while contraception turns people into bourgeois. I do not claim to agree with all these explanations. The fact remains that in 1958 propaganda in favour of the 'leap forward' replaced that in favour of birth control.

For some time there then occurred an extraordinary phenomenon. Rival teams hurled challenges at one another. Processions with flags and drums came to announce to the leaders of the campaign that their ambitious targets had been passed. The result was an inflation of statistics which was later corrected. Finally it had to be admitted that the 'leap forward' had also failed. Workers had exhausted themselves under the orders of incompetent leaders. The gathering in of the harvest had been neglected so as to ensure the functioning of blast-furnaces whose products had turned out to be worthless. Now the Chinese have emerged from the boastful doctrinal period to enter what Marshal Chen Yi modestly calls 'an experimental phase of ten years', characterized by the restoration of a certain degree of supply and demand, and the result will probably be an improvement in agricultural production. But China is still faced with the problem of her tens of millions of babies, and she will have to return one day, with more consistency and determination, to the rejected policy of birth control. If she refused to do so she would only start a new flight from totalitarianism, no longer just towards food and freedom, but towards contraceptives. (Today the whole of South Asia has been won over to them.)

At the moment the U.S.S.R. is saved from overpopulation by her vastness, her natural resources, the consequences of the war against Hitler, the birth control practised spontaneously in Russian families, and a radical rejection of all Chinese immigration. What is more, like the capitalist states, she distinguishes between her theory and her practice, reconciling medals for mothers of large families with a contraceptive policy sheltering under the banner of respect for women's health. Her demographic evolution reflects the events of her recent history more than her rulers' doctrine. Because of her losses in the war (and the slowness of her agricultural development) she suffered and is still suffering from a shortage of industrial manpower. Towards the end of the Stalin era one of the sights which used to astonish the Western visitor was that of squads of women employed on heavy work. He was tempted to write in his notebook: 'A country of slave widows.'

The United States, a country of the same demographic size with which the U.S.S.R. tends to compare herself, has obtained a large demographic start on her, thanks to the German invasion of Russia. Whereas since 1917 the American population has increased by 80 per cent, the population of the U.S.S.R. has increased by only 30 per cent. Mortality in Russia remains high, reflecting the backwardness of her civilization. It will probably fall in the future. If the rivalry between China and Russia increases, natalism will go on being advocated in the U.S.S.R. as a justification for the refusal to allow the surplus Chinese into Siberia. But comfort and a tendency to 'go bourgeois' will limit the success of this policy. And then the U.S.S.R. will be seen discreetly joining the advocates of a limitation of the world population.[7]

Certain theorists explain all historical development by variations in population. The economist Chan Ta, studying the history of China, divides it into cycles whose duration is in direct ratio to the intensity of demographic pressure. The triumph of a new dynasty produced peace and order, thus causing a rise in the birth-rate. But after a while the increase in population and the lack of inventions led to a certain saturation. Life became more and more difficult. In the end, plague, famine, and discontent brought about a revolution from which a new dynasty was born, and the cycle began again. This vision of a great tide of population advancing, withdrawing, advancing again, creating or sweeping away regimes, is certainly grandiose. But historical reality is made up of several categories of overlapping and inseparable phenomena.

It has been said that the France of 1789, with her twenty-five million inhabitants, was over the optimum of the time, that this fact may have had something to do with the outbreak of the Revolution, and that the situation was remedied by the wars of the Empire. But in opposition to this it must be pointed out that the most densely populated countries are not necessarily the most warlike: Holland is not the most bellicose nation in Europe. Overpopulation becomes a decisive war factor only with peoples of a certain temperament or a certain economic standard, when they are tempted by weak neighbours, etc. We must not try to establish a 'law'. All that we can reasonably say is that today the demographic phenomenon, amplified by the fantastic progress of medicine and more clearly revealed by research, tends to eclipse all the others. Political and economic doctrines interpret it; they no longer overshadow it. The governments of the U.S.S.R. and China may both call themselves 'Communist', but the differences in their populations and birth-rates are enough to set them apart, and indeed to set them against one another.

The Bible contains this piece of advice: 'Increase and multiply.' It was a precaution against the high mortality of the time. To overpopulate was to create a reserve to provide against the perils of bad weather or epidemics, just as one stocks food in a loft when a period of shortage seems imminent. Is mankind similarly creating a reserve to provide against some future catastrophe which it can feel approaching? Are the milliards of human beings coming into this world destined to make good the losses in a future atomic war? 'Foresight' of this sort would be absurd: it would be trying to provide against the consequences of a conflict which it would have helped to start in the first place.

This policy ought not to be attributed to the Christian churches. In a message dated 15 July 1961 His Holiness John XXIII merely expressed the opinion that there does not seem to be any definite connection between overpopulation and economic depression. This statement suggests that the Vatican is not fully informed, but it also suggests that if it were it would take that information into account in formulating its policy. The same year, Cardinal Gerlier, in answer to a question, stated that it is the duty of a couple not to beget more children than they can bring up decently. Some American bishops have made less sensible declarations on the subject. This is because Christianity has a natalist tradition which is all the more difficult to abandon in that Communism is making a show of going back to it. Between these two rival forces there is a sort of competition in optimism. The first does not want to appear less confident in God than the second is in man. This rivalry sometimes carries both sides far beyond their ideas. In the tropics the Communist mayor of an overpopulated district, recalling a conversation he had had with the bishop of his city, told me: 'We are in agreement on this subject, but only in private.' In public the bishop was for procreation and the mayor for increases in family allowances.

Birth control first struck the Christian Churches as a new form of the forbidden fruit, a victory of the doctor over the priest, an extension of the power of reason in an intimate sphere which had hitherto been shared between instinct and religion. Today the principle of birth control has been accepted, but Catholics and Protestants are divided about the choice of methods. Rome accepts *regulation* and rejects *control*. The first term covers only *natural* methods. The second also includes mechanical and chemical methods. Free-thinkers and Protestants alone (at least in theory) enter this prohibited territory.

A new spiritual force has appeared in our time: the demographers. They are usually thought of as austere statisticians, with no experience of the passions of the age. Nothing could be further from the truth. Their subject is concerned with the most profound and intimate aspects of human life, and what has drawn them to it is often an unconscious desire to free themselves from a complex or to give expression to a sensibility.

It would be amusing to classify them from this point of view. The male Malthusian could be presented as an introvert who hates the mob, cultivates aesthetic values, and refuses to change his habits; while the female Malthusian could be docketed as a feminist frustrated by the exhaustion of her political programme (votes for women, civil equality, and so on) who is trying to complete her emancipation by means of 'voluntary' motherhood. A few subdivisions could also be established: frigid, anxiety-ridden, crazy. I shall give examples only of these last two types.

William Vogt, the author of *Challenge to Survival*, is terrified that poetry and representative government may soon disappear, is afraid that the Maltese may run short of water, deplores the drop in the quality of bread, asks what is going to become of old cars, and thinks that a steak from an ox fed on plankton will taste fishy. These dangers are not all equally alarming or imminent. Richard Meier, the author of *Modern Science and the Human Fertility Problem*, after condemning on eugenic grounds the idea of a tax on children (which would indirectly penalize children already born), suggests encouraging sterility in those professions which already involve a certain amount of separation of man and wife: fishermen, pilots, doctors, nurses, artists, athletes, journalists, diplomats. Certain women workers, whose life is exhausting if they have children and terribly dreary if they are alone, could be both freed from motherhood and rewarded with wage increases (since the firm employing them would be sure of the continuity of their work). New family organizations would also be created, in which they would be given the function of 'aunts of honour', so as to enable them to come in contact with children. Meier insists that changes of this sort (some of which are already beginning to take shape) would not upset the life of the United States any more than military service, urbanization, and social mobility do now. Certainly serious overpopulation might lead to measures of this kind. But would it not be better to avoid that overpopulation than to copy its consequences in advance?

The natalists in their turn could be divided into extroverts, optimists, and misers. Extroverts? That goes without saying. The natalists want a lot of movement around them, want the house to be full, want 'things to happen'. Optimists? Yes, because they think that Nature will always end up by adapting herself to man's needs and instincts. Misers? That word seems paradoxical at first, for the natalist is prodigal with his sap, takes risks, incurs expense, etc. Yet an ancient fear is installed at the back of his mind: he is afraid of running out of human material. France, having just recovered from a crisis of underpopulation, is particularly alive to this danger. 'The Frenchman is becoming a rarity', wrote Giraudoux in 1939. The French demographic school was founded as a reaction against a century of 'Malthusian' practices. It inspired the system of family allowances and saw in the rise in the birth-rate a victory for its activity. When, later on, it turned to world problems it found it rather difficult to get rid of its habits. It did not dare tell the French on the one hand: 'Have more children', and the underdeveloped nations on the other hand: 'Have fewer'. Yet they would have been doing a service to the latter if they had done so.

The demographers today enjoy considerable power, and, as everyone knows, power corrupts. Communities come to consult them, just as an individual consults his doctor, and they hold their future in their hands. Alfred Sauvy, with his intelligence and sense of humour, must smile to himself when the Walloons, suffering from an inferiority complex with regard to the Flemings, ask him for a prescription. But he enters into the spirit of the game and solemnly tells them to fecundate their wives. Similarly a demographer can take any entity with a common characteristic (in this case the French language), point out its numerical inferiority to a neighbouring entity, and urge it to fill the gap. Then, in all probability, the neighbouring entity will try to go one better. Soon, as distrust spreads, the two associates will loosen the bonds uniting them, and later perhaps they will divorce. Today it is a question of Belgium, but the game could be started again tomorrow in Ireland. If a Catholic majority comes into existence in Ulster the whole province may slip under the control of Eire. Sauvy would therefore conclude that the Protestants must, as a matter of urgency, produce more children. On the other hand, one may imagine a Malthusian specialist advising the Walloons and the Orangemen to defend themselves by spreading contraception among the Flemings and the Irish. This, indeed, is what the Protestants are doing instinctively in certain parts of the world where they are in serious competition with the Catholics. The latter increase their numbers by employing only one, inefficient, method of birth control. This is unfair competition, say the Protestants, who counter with an equally unfair trick. Introducing their opponents to more modern methods of birth control is castrating them after a fashion.

Finally, let us mention a group of natalists which is small in number but considerable in influence. I shall not give their names, for I have nothing against them personally. I shall call them collectively 'the investors in men'. I use that term to refer to the intellectuals who need great human masses for the fulfilment of their schemes. These unscrupulous men treat labour as others treat money, and as their ideological investments are particularly profitable in overpopulated areas, they are eager to maintain exorbitant birth-rates in those areas. Generally speaking, they refuse to admit this. But it is possible to recognize them by their use of certain tricks and fallacies which I shall now try to enumerate.

1. *The use of the word 'Malthusianism' now in a demographic sense, now in an economic sense* (which was never intended by Malthus). In the writings of the 'investors in men' this word means now birth control, now restriction of production, disinvestment, deflation, etc. This confusion is systematically created so as to give the first term (birth control) an unfavourable connotation. True, the two types of phenomena may be linked together. But they are not bound to be. Between 1880 and 1940 France showed signs of economic and social conservatism which could be connected with certain cultural phenomena: the peasant concept of property, excessive legalizing, etc. Where was the cause, where was the effect? After considering the question in his book *Paix et guerre entre les nations*, Raymond Aron concludes: 'That demographic stagnation made conservatism possible is certain. That it made it inevitable is debatable. That in the absence of demographic growth a country is condemned to a low rate of economic development or to economic stagnation is not proven.'

2. *The presentation of every increase in population as a naturally beneficent phenomenon.* Yet it is not an increase in the total manpower but an increase in the educated, thrifty minority which adds to a country's wealth. It is not numbers but solvent demand that

rouses the spirit of invention. From the fact that at certain moments, in certain historical circumstances, a demographic increase constituted a favourable factor, it does not follow that the same will be true in other countries and in other circumstances. It is pointless to take into consideration a technique which exists somewhere else, but which the population in question is incapable of applying. Yet that is what our theorists do when they apply to the underdeveloped countries arguments based on observation of certain developed countries.

Even in the latter and in times of prosperity, an increase in population may present serious drawbacks. Britain, deprived of the naval supremacy which used to favour her commercial expansion, and incapable of feeding her own population, lives in perpetual dread of a deterioration of her balance of payments. Moreover the extension of trade, an advantage traditionally attributed to demographic expansion, can be just as easily obtained by the lowering of customs barriers and the integration of economies, as is shown by the example of the Common Market.

3. *The invention of a non-existent depopulation.* When signs appear of a fall in the birth-rate the individual and national instinct of self-preservation responds. The normal woman wants a child for her own physical fulfilment, and when she has one she wants another so that the first-born may have a playmate. In this way the necessary process of replacement occurs naturally. The State may encourage this process of replacement, but it has no need to enforce it by cultivating ignorance and disease. It was still widely believed about 1900 that most men and women, unless they were restrained by the fear of venereal disease and unwanted children (the 'two risks' of which Michel Corday spoke in a novel of the time), would become profligate and sterile. Experience has disproved this belief. A 'baby boom' occurred in the United States at the same time as the number of birth-control clinics was increasing and the venereal diseases were disappearing.

All sociologists agree that demographic expansion is a good thing in principle. A shrinking population would in the long run see its economy go into decline. The only debatable point is the *degree* of growth which is desirable. In the United States Malthusian authors recommend a reduction by one-third of the number of births. The population would then double in 140 years, instead of doubling in forty years as it will if the present rate of increase is maintained. There is therefore no question of stagnation. It can even be asserted that it is only in so far as the increase is slowed down that it will be able to continue and exercise its beneficial effects. At the present rate the country is rushing towards the danger which the natalists say that they dread most of all: a brutal attempt to remedy the situation, the age pyramid becoming a rectangle (as many old people as children), the demographic spasm.

4. *The exaggeration of the difficulties created by the ageing of a population.* Where the problem exists in an acute form, as the result of a sudden fall in the birth-rate—in Japan for example—it is really only a question of a temporary lack of balance, caused by the inevitable reaction to a previous state of overpopulation. For a certain period in the future more old people will have to be supported by fewer young people. But the latter will previously have been relieved of the crushing burden which too many children imposed on them. The main thing is to know whether in the meantime this 'unballasting' will have made possible the opening of a cycle of prosperity. If the answer is yes (in Japan this is already known to be the case) the material adjustment will be easy. The workers will be able to meet the expenses of the pensioners with considerably increased incomes. Why should an old Japanese be better supported by six sons, three of whom would remain wholly or partially unemployed (and would therefore also be dependent on the family), than by three sons with rising wages? In the underdeveloped countries this problem of an ageing population does not exist, at least for the State. The community builds the schools and pays the teachers; a rising birth-rate consequently means rising taxes. On the other hand there are no old-age pensions, so that the ageing of the population does not add to public expenditure.

5. *Rejection of the very term 'overpopulation'*. Population, we are told, can never be excessive except in relation to a certain level of subsistence. The real problem is that of raising the latter to the level of the former. The discovery of an oil gusher, for instance, is enough to justify an increase in population. This is only very partially true. In reality there has been scarcely any success in transforming the wealth created by oil into an effective improvement of the standard of living of the peasants in either the Middle East or Venezuela. 'North America', we are told again, 'was overpopulated in the time of the Indians. It now has a thousand times more inhabitants but it has ceased to be overpopulated.' And from that correct observation we are taken straight on to a false statement. 'Europe doubled or quadrupled its population, depending on the region, during the nineteenth century while at the same time raising its standard of living to a considerable degree; it therefore had no need to limit its population as Malthus maintained.' It should be remembered that this increase in population took place *at the same time as* a drop in the birth-rate and large-scale emigration to the New World. But for these two correctives, Europe would not have made the progress it did. Even with these correctives it suffered from overpopulation in the course of the nineteenth century. When a United Nations official, in a conversation with me in his office overlooking New York, disputed this statement, I said: 'Look out of the window. What do you see? A million Irishmen, Italians, and Puerto Ricans. New York was populated by Celtic and Latin famines.' And as he could find no answer to this, I added: 'Where is the virgin continent to which we could export a surplus of men today?'

On this subject of European overpopulation let us note the sober comment made by Alfred Sauvy, whom nobody would accuse of Malthusianism: 'The fall in the birth-rate in Western Europe could safely have occurred forty or fifty years earlier, provided that it had remained within reasonable limits. Economic progress would have been a little slower and less cruel as a result.' Admittedly it is more convenient to place the entire blame for the suffering of the workers in 1840 on the cruel employers. But in that case, why is that suffering recurring in present-day China? Let us rise above these partisan quarrels. Let us dare to recognize in overpopulation a phenomenon which is comparatively independent of economico-political regimes, and which, when it occurs, shows them all in a sinister light.

True, the population optimum, if one tries to fix it, becomes an elusive notion. But in the Ireland of 1850 or the China of 1960 it is a matter of ordinary common sense. In other cases, the optimum can be defined according to the aim it is hoped to achieve. If the chosen criterion is strictly alimentary, it is necessary to ask: 'How many human beings fed on a minimum ration can be physically kept alive?' But the question the civilized man will ask is this: 'How many human beings can be given a life which will not be entirely absorbed by the effort of survival?' These two questions produce very different figures. And aiming at the first optimum means in practice giving up the second.[8]

6. *The presentation of urbanization and industrialization as sufficient in themselves to reduce the birth-rate automatically.* The birth-rate does in fact tend to fall in urban and educated environments. But there is no parallelism between the curves of economic growth and those of falling birth-rates: several countries in Latin America are now giving striking proof of this. Urbanization, when it is not accompanied by industrialization, is, as we have seen, a 'concentration' of the problem rather than the beginning of a solution. Industrialization itself works chiefly through the educational progress which generally accompanies it. But this is a slow process, and if we had to confine ourselves to waiting for it to finish, we should soon find ourselves faced with a human tidal wave too powerful to control. The automatisms of socialist demographers are as illusory as those of the liberal economists of the eighteenth century, because, like them, they are too long-term.

7. *The substitution of theoretical problems of production for real economico-political problems.* Progressive intellectuals have a natural affinity with the cities where they live. Their minds cannot conceive problems except within an urban context. The Marxist analysis of social strata, established for industrial societies, is

unsuitable for the underdeveloped countries, which are generally largely agricultural. So an attempt is made to reduce them as quickly as possible (by industrializing willy-nilly) to the Procrustean bed whose dimensions are known. Assuming on principle that the independent peasant is backward, the progressive intellectual refuses to see that the landowners in the little countries of Western Europe are excellent technicians, that family cattle-breeding is the most efficient there is, and that the agriculture of capitalist America gives the highest yields in the world; and they imagine on the contrary collectivist miracles. This prejudice has recently led to some sensational blunders.

When I visited China in 1959 one of France's leading 'experts' had just left. He claimed to have found evidence of the 'leap forward' vaunted by Communist propaganda. As an ordinary observer, I for my part lost that illusion within a few days. In Shanghai and Canton I had my doubts when I saw the queues outside the foodshops and when I visited an exhibition where people were admiring meatless chops and cakes made of potato flour or turnip flour. Later I searched the country districts in vain for the miraculous harvest of which I had been told. Where had it gone? Into bigger rations? Consumption had fallen. For export? China had been unable even to fulfil her commerical contracts. Into stock? I could not see where. But what struck me most of all was the lack of conviction of the officials I questioned. One of them asked me with an anxious look: 'Are you satisfied with my explanations?' I asked another what he hoped for in the near future: comfort, leisure, holidays? I shall never forget the smile of humble longing with which he replied: 'A bit more pork.' A few months later the Chinese government owned up. The 'expert' had accepted figures (and faked figures at that) instead of observing facts. He had shut his eyes so as not to be forced to doubt his dreams.

8. *The invention of false biological laws.* Populations with a surplus are presented as being endowed with irresistible fertility. The contrary is the case: the natural fertility of the Indians is lower than that of the Europeans. J. de Castro has even gone so

far as to claim that a shortage of proteins favours reproduction. (It would therefore be sufficient to feed the undernourished to reduce the birth-rate.) This fantastic thesis, disproved by serious experiments, has been so skilfully spread that it can even be found in lectures given at the University of Paris. This is because it flatters the fatalism of the progressives: 'Increase production and the result will be an *automatic* fall in the birth-rate.'

9. *Underrating of the possibilities of direct action on the birth-rate.* The blind trust in human ingenuity which is shown when it is a question of finding means of subsistence gives place to a no less radical scepticism when it is a question of controlling human reproduction. Yet this problem, as we shall see, is not radically different from those which are solved every day in the field of economics. The study of motivation and the discovery of new means of communication between men are the keys to success in both fields. Moreover, recent investigations have revealed that even in profoundly traditional countries natalist resistance is much weaker than had been thought.

Two undeniable successes must command the attention of any observer: Japan and Puerto Rico. After the passing in 1948 of a law authorizing the termination of pregnancy in certain 'physiological or financial' conditions, the annual figure of births in Japan fell by a million in seven years. In Puerto Rico it was possible to deal with the problem in a less brutal fashion, by means of a combination of birth control, industrialization, and emigration to the United States. (Japan could not resort to this last remedy.) It is difficult in practice to distinguish the respective influence of these different factors, but it is certain that each of them encouraged the others. If there had been no emigration unemployment would have developed, slowing down economic progress. If industrialization had not developed at the same time as emigration we could not talk of a resurrection of Puerto Rico but only of the deportation of her inhabitants. If birth control had not taken root the future would still give cause for anxiety. Encouraged, transported, and sterilized at one and the same time, the Puerto Ricans have seen their standard of living improve rapidly. As early as the decade 1940–50 Puerto Rico led all the countries in the United Nations in the individual-income race. During the first years of that prosperity the birth-rate went on increasing. Then, as expected, the curve began to fall. It has not risen again, in spite of the considerable slowing-down of annual emigration. A middle-aged Puerto Rican told me: 'When I was young we had no hope.' In 1962 the 'insoluble' problem of 1940 seems to have been solved.

But Japan and Puerto Rico are countries which progressives and natalists do not generally choose to visit.

In fact, why is there so much thinly veiled hostility towards birth control, when in large areas of the world its extension would obviously promote the progress which the progressives claim to be seeking? The explanation is that uncontrolled copulation serves the imperialist purposes of the planners. The increase in population favours rapid transfers of power. The surge of young people serves as an excuse for political radicalism. The politicians speak in advance in the name of the young. They assert that the most intelligent policy is that which hurries fastest towards a future which is assumed to be inevitable. (It is indeed inevitable if nothing is done to guard against it.)

Yesterday people were natalists for their own sakes. They wanted to increase the numbers of their sect or their race. That reactionary attitude no longer enjoys much success in the big countries of present-day Europe. On the contrary, a 'leftist' natalism is developing in Europe which does not exercise its influence on the spot but in the 'Third World', where it encourages the overpopulation of the overpopulated, who are easier to form into masses. Cheated of the revolution which they expected to bring about in Europe (where, even among the Communists, Communism is now out-of-date), our progressives are trying to export it to the underdeveloped countries in order to impose it on us later from the outside, arguing that we are 'one world'.

. . . . .

The optimism of the natalists, I fear, often conceals a deep-seated scepticism as to the value of life. They want to maintain around each individual an incessant, urgent, almost hysterical atmosphere of competition in order to prevent him from thinking, because if he thought (so they believe) he would reject life. Desiccated minds project on to the whole of mankind their own inability to vitalize and ennoble existence. To escape from their apathy they drag us to the gaming table and invite us to risk the fearsome *banco* of overpopulation. In some of them it is possible to distinguish a sort of sadistic curiosity. They keep asking themselves: 'When there are twenty or thirty milliard human beings on earth how will they set about surviving? Won't they find some magnificent answer to that challenge?' They want to take the process as far as it will go, 'just to see'. But what we should see would probably be a succession of wars and crises which would hurl us back along the road we have come. Let us remain true to the 'sublime moderation' of the Greeks. Let us try to combine economic progress and the limitation of population, so that the latter promotes the former.

Four

WHOM TO SUPPRESS?

MAN has developed only by triumphing over other living creatures which, if he had not fought them, would have destroyed him: wild animals or bacteria. The victory won over these external enemies now obliges him to fight more actively against himself—against the invasion of children which would result from his sexual activity if he allowed it to produce its natural consequences. In every country in the world abortion is a sort of continuous massacre. This massacre is regrettable, but it has to be admitted that the full development of all the aborted embryos (more numerous in certain countries than new-born children) would make the already agonizing problem of overpopulation quite insoluble. The struggle of life against life is inevitable. All that one can hope for is that it will not employ methods which are too cruel. Since couples are destined to reject some of the children Nature offers them, it is better to carry out this elimination before conception. Abstinence and 'control', though not properly speaking murder, suppress possibilities of life. This filtering of possibilities is one of the characteristics of civilized man. It is the condition of a qualitative progress (thanks to education, thrift, hygiene) of which mankind is entitled to be proud.

At all times, among the countless candidates for life, only a small number have won through. In the past, epidemics made the choice. Wars and infanticides completed the selection. Today it is up to us, it is up to the family or society to perform this task. Since chance no longer helps us, why should we strike blindly as it did? Why should we not choose, among human beings, the best, and among the years of life, those most worth living? This is an attractive idea. However, mention of a choice inevitably causes embarrassment, for choices can always be called in question. Why this person and not that? Why keep this sick old man alive, instead of bringing a bonny child into the world? The old man becomes distrustful, feels unwanted, suspects his heirs of hankering after his fortune. He remembers the coconut-tree of the primitive tribes (those who could no longer climb it were put to death), the gas-chamber of the Nazis, the draught in which old people who take a long time to die have always been placed.

In a truly harmonious existence middle age would be extended as far as possible and old age reduced to a brief preparation for death. Experience has shown that by methodically exercising his physical and intellectual mechanisms man can delay by several decades the sclerosis waiting for him. Modern science provides old people for this struggle, with the equipment they lacked before, from false teeth to mnemonic techniques. Wound up like clocks, they start going again.

Affection is a very effective key. A few years ago a Rumanian aroused world-wide interest by asserting that he had discovered an elixir of youth. His claim appeared to be well founded. The process was tried in England and failed completely. Yet the doctor was no charlatan. In Rumania some old people whom nobody bothered about any more, suddenly placed at the centre of public interest, invited to take part in an important experiment, called upon to grow younger, had responded to this appeal by indeed growing younger. Similarly, in the United States, a big firm keeps its pensioners in good spirits by helping them to entertain one another on their birthdays. In France Armand Marquiset has founded the Little Brothers of the Poor, who invade attics and garrets on Easter Sunday to resuscitate with presents old people who are already half dead. All this is splendid, provided that we remember that it is a losing battle. Old age is essentially a gradual adjustment to death by way of a host of little experiences in which the person concerned, meeting growing resistance, realizes that life no longer suits him and ends up by resigning himself to losing it. Trying to fight too brilliantly against this decadence means aggravating the effect of the tell-tale shocks or of the final convulsion.

The fact is that modern society is not at all sure what to do with the human beings whose lives it prolongs. The old man of today is often demoralized because he feels in the way on this over-populated globe, and because he has secret doubts about the value of the extension he has been offered. Old age is at one and the same time a boon one longs for and a misfortune one tries to conceal. Those who reach it no longer feel, as old people used to, that they are sharing in the future through their descendants, because families today are smaller and less united. Homes are split up and grandparents only rarely live with their grandchildren. Thanks to the progress of longevity, the coexistence of several generations has become a common phenomenon, but it is no longer a real coexistence. Moreover, the respect which used to be shown to the 'elder' is denied to the old-age pensioner. The rapid change in living conditions has reduced the value of his experience. Nobody really believes in his wisdom any more. Old women too have become useless in their children's houses. Machines, hospitals, and schools do the work which used to be entrusted to them. Finally, the values of youth have been aggressively asserted in newspapers, films, and books. Those who used to leave early, but with royal honours, are presented with twenty years of discreet relegation. They feel frustrated by the civilization which has saved them.

To obtain a glimpse of the future let us go once more to New York. The children of the American 'baby boom' are destined to live three-quarters of a century, especially if they belong to the female sex. (The present expectation of life is sixty-seven years for men and seventy-four for women—but that is not the last word of medical progress.) Everything is done to feed, amuse, and care for those who are 'too old to work and too young to die'; this is one of the great tasks of the age. The idea that old people have a right to work is making progress, but it is difficult in practice to find a place for this work in industry and to give it some significance in the economy. There is talk of extending and renewing professional training, of introducing breaks in the activity of sexagenarians, of finding them work within their capacity, of postponing their retiring age, and of organizing a period of transition (comprising notably a reduction in overtime and the replacement of piece-work by time-work). But attempts to organize all this meet with opposition from other groups and with resisting circumstances. Whether or not there is an official age-limit it is difficult to find work for unemployed old people. Even Sweden—the kindest country with regard to the aged—is no exception. Young employers and young workers regard their elders with feelings which are a mixture of fear, contempt, and jealousy. They consider them incapable of adapting themselves to new working methods and out to exploit their retirement. The combination of a pension and a wage earns the disapproval of all who do not profit by it. In the United States a retired worker loses on an average two-thirds of his income. The unions would like him to lose not more than a third. Nobody suggests abolishing completely this lowering of economic status which consecrates the degradation of the person concerned. To improve matters it would be necessary to accept the principle of adapting the work to the man; in other words to recognize the existence of values superior to the work itself. Our civilization has not yet reached that point.

It does old people good to tell them that they are not old, even if this rosy propaganda is never entirely convincing. Above all they must be enabled to tell themselves that they are still useful to society. In Communist China, about 1955, they were given the job of killing flies. Elsewhere their activities are less degrading, but more often than not they are still fringe activities. Occupying the sexagenarians, amusing the septuagenarians, helping the octagenarians (when they are flagging) to die—this is what present-day society could do. In a little while it will be possible to delay this programme by one or two decades—to occupy the octogenarians, amuse the nonagenarians, and send the centenarians to heaven.

Unfortunately it does not seem that we can hope for anything better on this earth.

In the United States villages are built for old people where apartments are arranged round a central patio in order to encourage them to mix. Some social workers drag them from the benches where they tend to linger and make them play, dance, and swim until they die in the midst of general gaiety. Other less energetic helpers confine themselves to suggesting hobbies, and among these hobbies they make room for religion. But more often than not the golf club takes the place of the church and prayer disappears at the same time as work. Some people are indignant at seeing old people treated like children in this way. During a conference on the problems of old age, held in 1960 at the White House, an American rabbi made a passionate protest in the name of those concerned about spiritual values: 'There comes a moment in life when a man can no longer think in selfish terms, when he can no longer ignore these questions: Who needs me? Who needs mankind? How can I link up with an ultimate source of meaning?' Alas, at the very moment when only love could save him, the old man feels incapable of giving and receiving it. He has the impression of possessing a treasure but of being unable to pass it on. How can he share with others, across the differences in ways of life and the rapid evolution of language, the moments of inspiration which have marked his life? The generations will never be truly reconciled until the day comes—as, fortunately, it must—when, the 'momentum of history' having slowed down, a common denominator can be found. In the meantime there remain the infinite possibilities of solitude, and these are not incompatible with certain forms of communication. There are sexagenarian students today who, after a lifetime of specialized work, open their eyes to the wide horizons of human knowledge. Why should not tomorrow see a new blossoming of monasteries, some religious, others secular? Perhaps men may even come to long for retirement as the dawn of a better life.

If mankind finally makes a success of that difficult enterprise, growing old, and if it manages to breathe real life into its increasing population of retired workers, it will still have to temper that inevitable disaster: death. This problem is going to change in character. Vaccines and antibiotics, triumphing over smallpox and tuberculosis, have reserved modern man for coronory thrombosis and cancer, diseases which chiefly affect highly strung sexagenarians in civilized countries. But these diseases will be conquered in their turn. After successfully resisting all attacks, man will reach that advanced age when one dies from the 'difficulty of existing'. He will no longer be carried off in the midst of a busy life, but will fade away slowly after a nostalgic self-examination. A death like that, which people call gentle, is sometimes terrible.

In ancient Rome a court could, in certain circumstances, authorize voluntary death. Today the doctor, armed with an analgesic, can act as that court and carry out the sentence. But it is in his interest, as well as being his traditional 'duty', to prolong his patient's life at all costs. In that way he displays his virtuosity, makes money, conforms to the rules of his profession, and incurs no criticism. On the other hand, if he cuts short his patient's life, even with the latter's consent, he renders himself liable to prosecution. (Nobody is entitled to abet a suicide.) Now, it is unlikely that the patient will take the initiative. There are generally two distinct people in him. One of them, the more conscious of the two, wants to die. The other, the one who could take action to fulfil this wish, is prevented from doing so by fear, tradition, religious belief, or physical incapacity. A third person would be necessary to carry out the project, but—except in a few rare and tragic circumstances—that person is not available.

Yet euthanasia, an act of slight anticipation, is quite distinct from homicide and suicide properly so called. To throw in the towel because of a temporary setback, when the fight can still be won, is cowardice. But to shorten a death-agony is to show respect to a life approaching its close by sparing it a final humiliation which would spoil it. It is highly commendable to save a human life, if it is really the life of a *man* which is involved. The life of a creature which has reverted to the condition of an animal, or rather of a machine, does not deserve so much consideration. To reduce the fear of degradation would indeed mean removing a shadow which hangs over the end of human life. Man is born to act, believe, venture. Let us save him from that state of despair in which, as the body triumphs over the mind, he ceases to hope for recovery and can no longer sublimate his suffering. To shorten the transition is not to go against the divine plan, but to perfect it. To prolong a state of degradation, to pit oneself against an imminent and ineluctable death by misusing the resources of science—it is surely that which is an act of impiety.

It may be objected that no sick person is necessarily incurable. For the moment, alas, the number of incurables is growing. More people reach the age of the mysterious cancer. Other diseases leave still less doubt. Sometimes they give rise to heartbreaking incidents such as the Faita case which was recently tried in a French court. A man killed his incurable brother after doing everything in his power to cure him. He was arrested, imprisoned, tried. He told the court: 'I worshipped my brother. I made him a present of his death, a present which I know to be extremely expensive. I am ready to pay the price.' And a girl wrote to him from Italy: 'My fiancé is suffering from the same disease, but nobody loves him enough to kill him.' Before this, in a similar case, a priest came forward to plead for the 'guilty man'. The one to be pitied in cases like that is not the dead man (it would be more fitting to call him 'the released prisoner') but the person who has to assume the responsibility for his death. Whether he acts or refrains from acting, he will suffer remorse in any case. But a new morality is taking shape. In the last century euthanasia was still punished with death. Now the crime is down-graded to an offence, or else use is made of extenuating circumstances or a stay of execution. And juries obviously feel that this is still not enough, since the accused are often acquitted. In the past, under the pretext of prolonging life, people prolonged the death-agony with an easy conscience. That was buying virtue cheap. Today, for certain strict consciences, it is the act of prolonging (or initiating) an obviously undesirable existence that seems a crime.

Those who condemn euthanasia are fond of citing exceptions:

such and such a patient given up for lost was saved in the end. . . . Is that sufficient justification for all the suffering accepted, or rather inflicted, in the name of those exceptions? We are entitled to ask this question. But since different people will give different answers, let us adopt the most prudent solution. Any man who wants to survive must be helped to do so, even if his life does not strike us as worth living. It is only at the end of life, in the case of very old patients who are in great pain and begging for death (or no longer even in a condition to decide), that euthanasia—surrounded by precautions and guarantees—should be legally permissible. But perhaps this is still asking too much. When a broadcast on the subject was announced the French radio received congratulations from young people who were eager to get rid of their elders. If it is absolutely necessary to safeguard the rule which forbids any form of murder (with the possibility of a few discreet exceptions) let us at least know what our real motives are. We are afraid of abuses, or murder in disguise.

Before we make up our minds let us read once more the wise words of Pope Pius XII: 'The moral law naturally condemns the "well-meaning" murder, that is to say the intention of killing. But if a dying person so desires, narcotics may be used in moderation which will not only ease his suffering but also induce a speedier death. In this case death is not the direct intention.' One is in fact shortening the life in question, but one cannot be absolutely sure of this, or rather one refuses to know. Morphine solves these cases of conscience (just as the 'rhythm method', as we shall see later, solves others). But where exactly does the frontier lie between legitimate anaesthesia and criminal euthanasia? When does the death-agony begin? In our day there can only be different answers to this question, given by individuals in the half-light of their private consciences. My belief is that society will become less stringent in proportion as the precise duration of an existence is fixed less and less by Nature and more and more by the artifices of medicine. Then, obviously, the doctor who prolongs an existence beyond decent and reasonable limits will assume a serious responsibility. Is that not already true today in certain cases, and is it not time to recognize the fact? This is the first step we can expect the public conscience to take. Perhaps it will be recorded before long in the medical code.

Hitler discredited eugenics for a long time with his monstrous experiments. For fear of justifying such excesses, people prefer to dismiss the subject. The result has been a very real intellectual regression. Let us give one of many examples. In his interesting lectures on political sociology in the Paris Faculty of Law Maurice Duverger describes eugenics as 'a policy which tends to operate systematically to the advantage of the upper classes and to the disadvantage of the lower classes'. What is the notion of 'class' (with its well-known political overtones) doing in this field? Perhaps it would be helpful to recall the Greek etymology of the term 'eugenics'. *Eu:* good. *Gennan:* engender. It is therefore a question of studying methods of healthy reproduction. The word 'healthy' is too vague? Then let us simply consider cases which are beyond dispute.

Here again vocabulary and etymology can help us. There is a lot of talk nowadays about *teratogenic* products. *Teras:* monster. *Gennan:* engender. We have become capable of creating monsters artificially and we are awakening to the realization of this fact. In 1962 a tragic episode forced us to take a stand. A sedative distributed too easily to pregnant women to calm their nerves resulted in the birth of several thousand abnormal children, a third of whom died at birth. Should we mourn these deaths? Should we hope for more thumbless hands, more feet growing straight out of the trunk, more digestive tracts without bladders, more malformed eyes? A British medical review suggested terminating the pregnancies of all the women who had taken large doses of the criminal remedy. This appeal was ignored, but one of the mothers in question revived the debate by killing, after its birth and with the connivance of her family and her doctor, the child monster which she had engendered. Another mother, afraid of a similar mishap, crossed the seas in search of a state which would authorize her to have an abortion, and a Swedish commission found her sufficiently 'disturbed' to grant her this favour.

Should we protect monsters? The question is going to be asked more and more urgently. In the countries where it has already made considerable progress the fight against infant mortality is now faced with a final obstacle: the mortality in the first week of life, which remains comparatively high. To attempt to suppress it is to fight, boldly and directly, against natural selection, and hence to risk increasing the number of unsuccessful lives. It is estimated in the United States that out of 80,000 annual deaths of children aged under a month, 10,000 are due to congenital malformations. Saving them would mean helping subhumans to survive whose existence would probably be unhappy and whose reproduction would be undesirable. There are some circumstances in which the struggle for life becomes hard to distinguish from an attack on life. Must we, even then, go on with it? In the face of a question like that the usual reaction is to stammer and flee. Man does not want to know that Goya's monsters are inside him, that his genetic patrimony is even weaker than his individuality, and that he can jeopardize it for centuries with a second's carelessness. But eugenic awareness will develop as the subject of teratogenes is explored more fully. The Institut de la Vie, which has just been founded in Paris, can make a useful contribution to this work, provided it does not give a purely quantitative definition of the treasure it plans to defend. What is life? Cells? In that case it is the most commonplace thing in the world. What is admirable is organized life, in its superior forms and harmonious manifestations.

In the lecture on eugenics from which I have already quoted Maurice Duverger adds: 'Certain fanatics go much further, calling for the sterilization of individuals suffering from hereditary diseases or mental ailments.' Is Maurice Duverger unaware that this sterilization is practised in highly civilized countries? During the first half of this century 50,000 Americans of both sexes (a third of them in California) underwent it. Finland, Norway, and Switzerland have followed this example. In Denmark there were over 8,000 cases of sterilization between 1929 and 1954. In that country castration is also practised; this is done without the consent of the man concerned if he is a mental patient, and if he is a sexual offender he is persuaded to give his consent by the offer of a reduction of his sentence. Such practices do not necessarily imply the creation of real human stud-farms devoted to the multiplication of superior individuals, to which Maurice Duverger refers in the same sentence. We cannot easily define 'superior individuals'. The appearance of a genius is often recognized only after a long period, too late to make it possible to 'stockpile his sperm'. And in any case there is no evidence that the sons of geniuses are bound to be geniuses themselves. On the other hand, we can define monsters and we should therefore prevent these individuals from harming, by propagating their taints, future individuals who will act as carriers, and hence society as a whole. To reject sterilization out of hand because the Nazi barbarians abused it is to adopt a passive attitude (in a spirit of contradiction). This is in itself barbarian.

In our present state of knowledge eugenics cannot be anything but purely negative. Even on this level great caution is advisable and indeed essential. In the United States there exist 'heredity advisers'. They act with extreme timidity for fear of incurring legal responsibility. Even when they are absolutely convinced that their client should not beget children they confine themselves to drawing his attention to certain books or statistics; and if he presses them to advise him what to do they reply: 'Try your luck.' This semi-authorization is just what their client was hoping for. The interview has eased his qualms of conscience, and off he goes, with his adviser's tacit complicity, to put into human circulation, for several centuries, harmful genes. In these conditions it is impossible to hope for (or fear) the complete elimination of hereditary diseases. But the sterilization of carriers of *dominant* bad genes could well be adopted on the lines of American and Scandinavian practice. This measure is often quite wrongly described as cruel. On the contrary, the persons concerned are generally relieved at being able to lead a normal sex life without being afraid that this will involve them in heavy responsibilities. Investigations carried out in one of the American states where sterilization is practised seem to show that among those sterilized there is a high percentage of happy marriages and successful social adjustments.

Nowadays we tend to underestimate heredity. We shall come to appreciate its importance more readily as differences in environment are reduced by the levelling of classes and the progress of communications. Eugenics triumph all around us in the spheres of agriculture and breeding. The vegetables, fruit, eggs, and meat that we eat are the results of genetic improvements. To claim that man is utterly incapable of making similar progress is to situate him in arrogant isolation in the midst of Nature, and hence to rebel against the whole course of modern science. What limits the value of this comparison is the fact that man is unwilling to undergo the treatments he inflicts on animals and vegetables. There is a vicious circle here: We cannot learn quickly except by experimenting and we know too little to be able to experiment safely. Already, however, certain findings have been made. Longevity is often hereditary. Biochemical functioning, metabolic activity, blood groups, morphological forms, and predispositions to certain diseases vary according to natural environments. The same is probably true of certain aptitudes. Racialism will one day find a serious scientific basis. But it will be a much more subtle theory than the one which is now known by that name. It will no longer be a question of the absolute superiority of all the members of one racial group over another, but of differences between the average types of each of these groups, which will give no reason for believing in the superiority or inferiority of any individual, nor even of any group as a whole.

Pending this advance, let us be cautious in taking action. In any case, the dangers of 'genetic erosion' have been grossly exaggerated. It is certain that medical progress is hindering the process of natural selection. But a certain amount of selection is none the less being made by social means: abnormal human beings reproduce less than normal individuals, for they are less sought after as partners in the game of reproduction. As for the consequences of radiation produced by atomic tests, they do not seem to be alarming as yet. The most obvious result of the agitation which these tests have aroused is to have drawn attention to the more serious risks which we had been running before when having X-rays at the doctor's or the dentist's.

All these spectres distract public attention from indisputable dangers and applicable remedies. I call the danger of over-population indisputable because it is already apparent and is certain to grow worse. The nuclear danger itself, if it materialized, would only be a by-product. For, in all probability, in an eventual conflict, the H-bomb, or hydrogen bomb, would be set off by the P-bomb, or population bomb.

Let us sum up. In a searching examination of the reasonable possibilities offered by modern science we have found only the means of relieving mankind of a few old people (expedited more rapidly), tainted individuals (sterilized), and monsters (suppressed).

To cut the population slightly at both ends and devote greater attention to the rest is not an unimportant objective from the point of view of human dignity. Life and death are badly distributed at the moment in our civilization. Thousands of lives are casually jeopardized out of sheer avarice. (I am thinking of the victims of industrial injuries or occupational diseases.) Pharmaceutical firms and cigarette manufacturers (who are sometimes state-controlled) put noxious products on the market and, if sales are good, are in no hurry to withdraw them from circulation when their harmful effects are revealed. The money spent keeping patients alive who are incurable and in pain is in practice taken from others who are curable—for men are always fighting over a blanket which is too short to cover them all. Sometimes the solution is even left to luck. I have heard of a doctor who now and then switches off the electric current of the iron lungs of his polio patients, to give them a chance to die or to survive (as the

Spartans did when they exposed their children to the elements). Our intellectuals give very little thought to all this. On the other hand, they try to rouse society's indignation over the execution of a few hardened criminals who, if they were put back into circulation, might kill innocent people. Has not the time come for a better distribution of charity?

Let us hope that this may come about. But that is not the way in which we can expect to find a solution to the demographic problem under consideration. This observation brings us to the central part of our study: that which is concerned with birth control.

Five

BIRTH CONTROL

BETWEEN the two wars Edward Himes published a history of contraception. It begins with an Egyptian papyrus of 1850 B.C., continues with Chinese herborists' recipes, gets lost in the darkness of the Middle Ages, reappears at an artisan level in the eighteenth century, and goes through its political revolution in 1877 (the trial of Annie Besant) and its industrial revolution about 1930 (the vulcanization of indiarubber). Since the publication of this work the practice of birth control has spread enormously. The term itself, especially when translated into other languages, lends itself to misinterpretation. It suggests control by the State, official intrusion into family life, when in fact it refers to control by families themselves. They are given help from outside, but this is only to enable them to exercise their free will. Use of the English expression in non-English-speaking countries has the advantage of recalling the Anglo-Saxon, Protestant, feminist origins of the movement. This movement had a heroine in the United States whose story deserves to be remembered.

Margaret Sanger derived her fighting spirit from her father, a tombstone sculptor and amateur philosopher who never tired of telling his children that man should devote his stay on earth to making it a better place. He tried to do this by fighting for votes for women and against Catholic immigration.

A suffragette from birth, Margaret Sanger delivered her first public speech, in a Methodist church, on 'Women's rights'. In those days people were already almost prepared to grant woman the right to choose her destiny as a citizen, but not her destiny as a mother. Becoming a midwife, Margaret Sanger found herself confronted with clients who were searching desperately for a means of spacing out the births of their children. The doctors, out of fear or ignorance, refused to answer them. Margaret Sanger could understand the anxieties of these exhausted mothers all the better in that she soon found herself in the same situation. After her third child she was advised not to have any more; she had already spent long months in a sanatorium. An incident in her professional life was to make a deep impression on her. She was called twice, at three months' interval, to the bedside of a woman who had aborted herself in a poor district of New York. The second time it was too late: the woman died in her arms. In the interval the doctor had given her no advice except to make her husband sleep in the attic. Henceforth, Margaret Sanger was to devote all her energies to fighting this murderous modesty. That would be her mission, her way of 'leaving the earth a better place after her stay on it'.

Rebuffed by the doctors she approached, disappointed by the books she consulted, she decided, after searching in vain through the libraries of New York, to go to Europe, where she had been told that birth control was practised. She visited England, France, and Holland, finding in their big cities some of the features which had shocked her in the United States: unhappiness among the women, hypocrisy among the middle classes, ignorance among the doctors. France, however, struck her as a highly civilized country, where mothers handed down to their daughters, at the same time as cookery recipes, contraceptive recipes. In Holland she learnt something essential: the unrestricted sale of contraceptive products was not enough—it had to be complemented by the creation of clinics where the women could learn how to use them.

The clinic which she founded in 1916 in a little two-room apartment in Brooklyn was very humble, but clients came flocking to it straight away. On the ninth day the police burst in and took everyone off to the police station. Some time before, after the publication of a pamphlet which was condemned as obscene, Margaret Sanger had had to go into exile to escape prosecution. This time she spent thirty days in prison with thieves and prostitutes. But the result was a great propaganda victory. Her sister, imprisoned at the same time, went on a hunger strike, and this touched tender hearts and led to a public meeting at Carnegie Hall. When she was released Margaret Sanger was greeted at the prison gates by a crowd of grateful women, to the strains of the *Marseillaise*. A new era was beginning in which, for the advocates of birth control, imprisonment was no longer a threat but an aim. (Today, in reactionary Massachusetts, it is they who ask to be arrested, and their Catholic adversaries who refuse them this favour.)

With powerful backing, Margaret Sanger set out to have the American law altered. In 1936, as a result of her campaigns, the law prohibiting doctors from giving advice on birth control was abrogated, and as early as 1937 the study of contraceptive techniques was put on the curriculum of the medical faculties. Margaret Sanger had already extended her activity abroad. Lecture tours took her to the China of Chiang Kai-Shek, to India, and to the U.S.S.R. Just after the Second World War General MacArthur, afraid of being accused of genocide, prevented her from landing in Japan. But it was already too late to prevent the triumph of the movement. Today, at the age of eighty, Margaret Sanger is a world-famous figure of whom America is justly proud.

In Britain the number of birth-control clinics has grown considerably. There are 358 in England, most of which are installed in hospitals and dispensaries and form part of the municipal health services; 250,000 people are given treatment or advice in them every year. In just one district of New York (Manhattan) there are five. Women come to them without shame or fear, with children whom they leave to play in the waiting-room. Each woman's case is studied, the method which seems most suitable is recommended to her, and the necessary product is sold to her at a discount.

The movement's victory remains incomplete. We must not imagine whole populations trained in the use of mechanical or chemical contraceptives. Even today Monsieur de Grignan, Madame de Sévigné's son-in-law, remains the typical figure in the matter of birth control. I say 'Monsieur de Grignan' because we have a remarkable document on him which belongs to literature. Madame de Sévigné writes: 'Listen to me, son-in-law. If after this boy you do not give your wife a rest I shall assume that you do not love her. . . . I shall take your wife away from you. Do you think that I gave her to you to be killed, to have her health and youth destroyed?' Two months later the Marquise intervenes once more. This time she writes to her daughter: 'I am beginning to think that it is time to remind Monsieur de Grignan of the promise he has made. Remember that this is the third time you have given birth in November. It will be September next time unless you control him.' In reality it is Madame de Sévigné who 'controls' him from a distance, with that additional zeal which comes from jealousy. Finally Monsieur de Grignan, utterly cowed, obeys, and his mother-in-law congratulates him. 'I am delighted, my dear daughter, that you are not pregnant. I love Monsieur de Grignan for this with all my heart. Tell me if I owe this happiness to his temperance or to his real affection for you.' Temperance? Nowadays we should say: rhythm method. Affection? Probably we should read: *coitus interruptus*.

To write the real history of contraception would be to list a long succession of marriages broken by feminine spite or masculine frustration, to describe departures from an over-fruitful bed to the hateful isolation of the separate room or to the substitute of an adulterous relationship. Literature appears to have decided, once and for all, to ignore the subject, so that its descriptions of sexual relations remain conventional. A few recent investigations (mainly American) have begun to clear this jungle of its undergrowth. In them we discover man in his entirety, with his complexes, his fears, his social ties, his religions. Kinsey had already taught us that the poor are more continent, more modest, and quicker to take their pleasure. Since then, Lee Rainwater has carried out a more searching investigation and obtained some revealing confidences.

A couple who both go out to work have different working hours. The man comes home and wakes his wife. Although she is neither physically nor mentally ready, she does not want to frustrate him, but during their intercourse she remains tense and frigid, and what she really feels is not the pleasure which she appears to be taking but fear of the pregnancy which will follow. The woman who recounted that spoke for millions of others. In all the primitive forms of contraception one of the partners sacrifices himself, either the man in spoiling his pleasure or the woman in accepting its consequences. More enlightened couples plot together to obtain both pleasure and immunity. Or else each partner tries to throw responsibility on to the other which in the end neither accepts. Grave moral problems are tacitly settled in a second, in a state of passionate emotion. Alfred Sauvy tells this story: 'An American doctor, consulted by a father of four who was finding it extremely difficult to bring them up, advised him to think hard, at the moment of orgasm, about his financial resources and the number of children he was capable of feeding. A little while later the father came to announce his wife's fifth pregnancy. "Didn't you follow my advice?"—"Yes, I did, but at that moment I had the feeling I could feed a vast number of children." '

The man counts on the woman to take precautions in order to save him the trouble of having to discipline himself. Yet he hopes that she is not too well informed on the subject: if she were would it not be easier for her to deceive him, since she would no longer fear the consequences of her adultery? To leave her ignorant and afraid is to attain at smaller cost the aim pursued by the Chinese in binding his wife's feet, and by the Moslem in inflicting the torture of excision on her. It is a way of safeguarding his right of ownership, of avoiding comparison, of remaining the one god of a slave wife.

In refusing to spoil his pleasure the male is defending a brief moment of illusion in which he escapes from his human condition.

This moment enables him to go back to past ages and rediscover a bygone awareness. He experiences an intense pleasure in acting and, even more, in being acted upon. He merges into a great germinal tide, with no age or individuality; he partakes of the communion of life. Kierkegaard once wrote: 'The loftiest passion of thought is to discover something that it cannot think.' Sex answers this demand. It is like a reservoir of madness into which hypercivilized people are happy to escape from their world of steel and glass. In it they give free rein to feelings or ideas: the cult of beauty, love of one's partner, the fusion of the couple, the hope of extension by conception. The orgasm is the springboard of these transcendental experiences. A man who merely relieves himself of his sperm feels remorse as a result. He has missed a chance of worshipping, of giving, of creating, of initiating himself in a dark and magical past, or of living to the end of time, down a long line of descendants.

In Chapter xxxviii of Genesis we read: 'Judah took a wife for Er his firstborn, whose name was Tamar. And Er, Judah's firstborn, was wicked in the sight of the Lord, and the Lord slew him. And Judah said unto Onan: "Go in unto thy brother's wife, and marry her, and raise up seed to thy brother." And Onan knew that the seed should not be his; and it came to pass, when he went unto his brother's wife, that he spilled it on the ground, lest that he should give seed to his brother. And the thing which he did displeased the Lord; wherefore he slew him also.' This is a story rich in meaning. Although (in respect to the marriage law) Onan's action is highly moral, it is regarded here as criminal. The prejudices which even today surround masturbation show that this judgement corresponds to a profound masculine instinct. A man does not indulge in solitary pleasure without feeling regret for the complete fulfilment of which he is only a caricature.

The demographers pay scant attention to this intimate psychology. Yet it influences their statistics. In practice, man strives to reconcile contradictory desires. He must always choose, to a certain extent, between emotion and discretion, premeditation and surprise, forgetfulness and safety. Civilized people tend to prefer discretion, premeditation, and safety, but not without regretting what they are losing. The Russian biologist Pavlov made his name with experiments which unbalanced animals by associating the sight of food with a sharp electric shock. In *coitus interruptus* the wretched human frog finds himself similarly torn between the promise of pleasure and the threat of poverty. We find Casanova in the eighteenth century already complaining at having to 'shut himself up in a piece of dead skin in order to prove to himself that he was perfectly alive'. For women, local chemical methods have a major drawback: they have to be used before intercourse. This, as an American doctor pointed out to me, compromises the whole mechanism of their coquetry. It has always been understood that it is the man who attacks and the woman who may or may not surrender. She loses this tactical advantage if she lets it be known that she has foreseen her capitulation in advance. The contraceptive pill suits her better, because it enables her to make a clear distinction between the sexual act and the precaution which nullifies it. Passionate at one moment, calculating at another: this ambiguity appeals to her. But in other ways, as we shall see, this pill is the most intimate of attacks on her feminity.

Although it has become more conscious, more socialized, the 'moment' retains a sacred character. To experience it fully together is the couple's profound desire. To help each other to do this is one of the forms which their love assumes. But there are a great many individual differences, a great deal which cannot be shared between the two partners. The passing moment is infinitely precious for one, commonplace for the other. Yet they must come to an understanding in order to live it together, in a combination of charity and commerce. These misunderstandings are, it seems, disappearing. Freer morals and a better knowledge of sexual techniques have reduced the number of frigid women. Yet there remains an irreducible psychological residue of *outsiders* who refuse to admit that this is what they are and put on a show of participation, or else, embittered by their disappointment, turn into prudes or spurious mystics. Some of them, seeing that they have nothing to lose, do not hesitate to cut short the pleasure of the male, pleading the excuse of 'control'. Perhaps they are secretly jealous of him. Others, on the contrary, are the victims of this interruption: they had not yet reached their own climax.

Sometimes petty considerations enter into the problem. The couple are not rich and have to choose how to spend their money. The man buys spirits for himself instead of buying contraceptives for his wife. Or else she wastes the product out of carelessness. Then unsuccessful attempts are followed by dangerous abortions—until, in some cases, final relief is obtained through sterilization. The astonishing thing is that all this takes place in silence. Husband and wife scarcely ever speak to each other about these questions. Yet they long to talk about them, and when a third party broaches the subject they jump at the opportunity. The most difficult thing, say the American investigators, is not getting people to talk but getting them to stop talking. These investigators discovered to their surprise that each partner in a couple, questioned separately, attributed to the other a point of view which he did not in fact have. People can be too close together to know one another.

In huge areas of the world life is still steeped in magic. Certain social or religious practices are, as we have seen, methods of birth control. Others act in the opposite direction. Thus in India there is a taboo which prohibits sexual intercourse during precisely that first week in the menstrual cycle when it could take place without any consequences. This taboo, which perhaps reflects a clumsy search for a safe period, in fact reduces the margin of safety. Or else, if the two partners consult both the magician and the doctor and observe both periods, they are parted for ever.

I described Monsieur de Grignan earlier as the typical figure in the field of birth control. That was giving too much credit to modern man. Sophisticated people, armed with condoms and diaphragms, smile at those natives on Trobriand Island who are ignorant of the causal relationship between sexual intercourse and conception. But they themselves are only a minority. A great many men alive today have not yet become fully aware of this relationship, at least in its precise form: the connection between the emission of sperm and ovulation. Consequently they do not know the technique, which we believe to be primitive, of *coitus interruptus*. Monsieur de Grignan was therefore something of a pioneer. His gesture implies a remarkable effort of analysis, invention, and self-control. Though it has become commonplace in the West, it was originally revolutionary. It is one of the great achievements in the history of mankind. Whole peoples are still living in ignorance of it.

The 'family planners' have almost everywhere come up against elementary difficulties which they had not at first foreseen. Most women prove incapable of remembering a date or counting days.[9] World overpopulation reflects to a great extent the human race's failure in this humble examination in arithmetic and attention. Disappointed, the Malthusians transferred their hopes to a miraculous pill which should solve the problem entirely. In 1950 Margaret Sanger went to see Dr. Pincus, the expert on the endocrine glands, and suggested that he should try to discover a contraceptive. After a lengthy study of woman's reproductive cycle Pincus found that the pituitary gland was the source of a secretion circulating in the blood which led the ovary to produce an egg. If this communication could be cut ovulation would not take place.

For a few years Pincus experimented on doe rabbits to determine women's future. The result of his research was the discovery of a pill, the sale of which was officially authorized in the United States in 1960, under the name of Enovid. Another pill is already selling in competition with Enovid, and the prices are falling. In the United States a woman can be sterile for two dollars a month. (In Britain the cost may be borne by the National Health Service.) The consequences of the use of the pill have been systematically studied in various places, above all in Puerto Rico. Among the women treated certain physical disorders were noticed, similar to those of pregnancy. But the researchers succeeded in proving that some of these disorders were, if not imaginary, at least psychic, for they also occur when placebos are substituted for the pills. However, a certain caution is recommended in the use of the pills. 'Not more than two years', says the prospectus. Why two years? This in fact represents a compromise between vague anxieties about the future and a desire for immediate contraceptive efficiency.

What might happen after the period of two years? First of all, a certain virilization of the woman. (Already hairs have appeared.)[10] Some specialists, arguing by analogy from other experiments with hormones, suspect the pill of a capacity to cause cancer. But its defenders claim on the contrary that it can act as a safeguard against cancer. Gratuitous accusations have been answered with hasty statistics. In our present state of knowledge both assertions seem mistaken. On the one hand, treatments with progesteron (a constituent element of the pill) have been carried out for quite a long time without any ill-effects being noticed. On the other hand, there would be no justification at present for using the pill as a preventive against cancer. A serious study of the question has only just begun. An investigation involving two separate groups of women (one group taking pills and the other not) is being carried out in Puerto Rico. It will not be possible to draw conclusions from it for a few years, and even then they will be dubious and provisional.

The pill intervenes in a very complex hormone process. It contains elements which, apart from the woman's sex, can affect her growth, her lactation, and her future children. These elements are in small proportions and have so far caused no catastrophes. But what is going to happen in the future? This solidarity raises fears of disturbing the whole feminine organism by intervening artificially at this central point. 'A pill which can be so useful,' many women argue, 'may also be very harmful.' Before using it systematically they would like to know all its effects. This discovery appears in the guise of the final fruit of the tree of knowledge, placed under an ancient Biblical curse. It will take a long time for a fear of this sort to be entirely dispelled, if it ever is. At the moment it is growing. In the spring of 1962 a connection was thought to have been discovered between use of the pill and certain thromboses. This suspicion was enough to lead to the banning of Enovid in Norway. At the same time a journalist asked some 'Malthusian' doctors gathered together at a congress in Warsaw: 'Would you give the pill to your daughter?' Most of them replied: 'No.'

One important point seems to have been established: the pill is more efficient than the other contraceptive methods. But only provided it is used properly, that is to say for twenty days a month. Here we once again come up against the difficulties of arithmetic and attention which make the rhythm method so difficult to apply. Now, if it is not used correctly, the pill too becomes more or less ineffective. One consequence of this fact has not yet been fully shown. According to certain statistics, after the treatment has been interrupted, the woman becomes pregnant more easily than before. If this is the case it may be doubted whether use of the pill will finally result in a reduction of the birth-rate. A pill whose use can only be temporary and imperfect, and which later produces an increase in fertility, makes it possible to space out births, not to limit the final complement of the family. Finally let us note that this remedy, intended for use in Asia, raises curious problems there: if it interrupts lactation the last-born child risks dying of hunger.

A solution to all these difficulties will probably be found one day. We are as yet only in the earliest stages of a new technique. We have started interrogating Nature, calling her in question, looking for the weak points in the mechanism of reproduction. They exist, and therefore we shall make progress. However, it is unlikely that we shall ever develop a perfect pill, which it would be enough to take only once a month. Any oral remedy is weakened as it passes through the body: consequently it has to be repeated frequently. In that case, what other methods can be tried?

Manufacturing anti-bodies? (There are some women who produce them spontaneously.) Stopping the emission of sperm? Preventing the egg from attaching itself to the wall? The later the intervention is made, the more it is ill-advised. The motivation becomes more powerful, but the operation bears a closer resemblance to murder. The best news would be the discovery of a sure and easily perceptible sign of the beginning of ovulation. A new rhythm method could then be determined, using an absolutely safe period beginning three or four days after the appearance of this sign and extending to the end of the menstrual cycle.[11] A discovery of this sort is not impossible, for ovulation is linked with the general endocrine equilibrium and must therefore correspond to other modifications.

'By her opposition to mechanical and chemical methods,' an ecclesiastic once told me, 'the Church will lead the doctors to find a much more satisfactory method.' Let us hope so, not forgetting that the problem is now an urgent one. To delay by one generation the application of existing methods under the pretext that better methods may be invented would be to accept a new doubling of the world population and to run the risk of an explosion.

The various aims pursued by contraception are not always entirely compatible. The spacing out of births is desirable in the interests of the woman's health, but it is not so desirable for the children, who will grow up separately, at different ages. The method which women prefer is sterilization, because it is final and removes all responsibility. (Irresponsibility is what most human beings want above all else.) You marry, you let the children come, and when you have had enough you call a halt. In Puerto Rico, where twenty per cent of the women are sterilized, *la operacion* has even become a social distinction. Women flock from the neighbouring islands to acquire this status symbol. But sterilization too is not an entirely satisfactory method, either from the individual point of view, because it is irreversible, or from the social point of view, because it is generally carried out too late, after several births, and therefore has only a limited demographic effect.

We must beware of being too doctrinaire on the subject. The practice of birth control is influenced by all sorts of individual and social factors. In Shaw's *Pygmalion* Professor Higgins maintained that an Englishman's education and career could be deduced from his pronunciation and his vocabulary (Eton-Oxford-India). Similarly one could, with occasionally a few uncertainties, draw portraits of couples based on their contraceptive practices. *Coitus interruptus*: an English couple perhaps, certainly not an American couple. Exclusive use of the rhythm method: a couple of ardent Catholics or backward peasants? Sterilization: this could be the case of a disciple of Simone de Beauvoir, an enemy of motherhood, or of a pious woman who wants to 'sin only once'. A condom? This indicates a ladies' man, or the husband of a selfish, lazy woman. A diaphragm? This is the sign of a submissive wife, or of a coquette anxious to afford her partner pleasure which will reflect credit on her.

In theory it is possible to adapt the whole range of contraceptive products to the various stages of life. The first stage will be that of the condom. The young girl must not be too knowledgeable: accordingly her parents will not give her any instruction, counting on her first lover to take the necessary precautions. (But is this trust justified?) Later on, the young bride, before going off on her honeymoon, will go to see her doctor who will give her a box of pills. (But this method is not advisable for young brides who have not yet finished growing, and besides, in order to be effective, the treatment has to start *before* marriage.) On her return it will be the right moment to fit a diaphragm. (But this method does not suit all women.) Finally, when three children have been born, the family will be brought to a stop by sterilization. (But the sterilized woman, after being divorced or widowed, may want to give her second husband a child; she will be unable to do so.) It is difficult to imprison a human life within a plan.

From the financial point of view, sterilization of the male is the best method: it calls for neither hospitalization nor immobilization. But it is also a definitive choice, made in the context of a situation which may later change. What is more, in many people's eyes it is a sacrilegious act. Primitive peoples imagine a single great river of sap flowing through men, animals, and plants. To interfere with human seed is to compromise the renewal of vegetation, for there exists a solidarity between all the forms of life. Among civilized peoples these superstitions change but do not disappear. The phallic cult remains in India, 'machism' in Spanish America. Even today, in the Puerto Rican districts of New York, mothers can be seen exposing, discussing, and extolling their little sons' sexual organs. A man thinks that he can prove his virility by the number of his children: a ludicrous idea, since a single emission contains enough spermatozoons to populate the whole of Europe. This boastful father is like a millionaire proudly displaying a few small coins. But here we are not in the realm of reason.

The Catholic position was defined in a text by Pope Pius XI, dated 31 December 1931, which authorizes married couples to use the safe period (during which, every month, a woman is naturally sterile) if there is a moral justification for doing so. This is a very different position from that of St. Thomas Aquinas, who regarded any carnal act which could not result in generation as an unnatural vice. Pius XII was even more precise in 1951: 'Serious reasons, such as those to be found in medical, eugenic, economic, and social reports, may exempt a couple for a long period, and even for the entire duration of the marriage, from the duty of procreation.' And on the same day he added: 'We assert the lawfulness and at the same time the bounds—in fact very wide bounds—within which a regulation of reproduction may be exercised which, unlike birth control, is compatible with the law of God. It may even be hoped that science will succeed in providing this legitimate method with adequate scientific bases.' A scientific discovery may therefore abolish in the near future the 'technical' basis of the Catholic position. It seems paradoxical that fundamental values should be dependent on such a contingent event. In fact the Church's present position consecrates a compromise, which became necessary at a certain moment in social evolution. The origin of this change was the trial of Annie Besant, which in 1877 sparked off a strong movement in favour of birth control. Priests started coming to terms with their feminine penitents in the secrecy of the confessional, and in 1931 Pius XI consecrated their practice by authorizing the 'rhythm method'. (A similar adjustment was to be made more rapidly in 1956, when, after three years of uncertainty, Pius XII authorized 'painless childbirth'.)

Today a new stage has to be covered, because the demographic problem has become more acute and because the methods of 'control' have developed. Consequently the Church no longer merely allows the use of the rhythm method but actively propagates it. By setting Catholic 'regulation' against Protestant 'control', she is giving the former considerable publicity. Today there actually exist some 'Catholic clinics' (one of which is called 'Happy Homes') and this adjustment in vocabulary is significant. But to state dogmatically that the rhythm method obtains just as good results as the other methods (as Father Riquet did recently) is an oversimplification,[12] and to confine oneself to preaching chastity is to show a deplorable tendency to avoid the issue. I have read a Catholic pamphlet which proposed solving the problem of Moslem overpopulation in Algeria by continence. Was this meant to be taken seriously? Virtues and vices are curiously juxtaposed in these debates. People serving a lofty ideal are not afraid to enter into an alliance with negligence, selfishness, and sometimes cruelty. Early marriage has the approval of the Church: it is a guarantee against debauchery. But in our times the return to this ancient custom is encouraged by the spread of birth-control methods. (Young people know that they can marry without being promptly burdened with children.) Similarly the fight against excessive fertility is bound up in practice with the fight against sterility. The two enterprises have progressed *together*. Both of them are helping us to a better knowledge of the mechanism of reproduction, so that we may be able to stop it or set it in motion according to physiological or social circumstances. The woman who, because she knows a method of preventing her pregnancies, has given up interrupting them, avoids the sterility which often follows abortion. She therefore continues to belong to the group of fertile women, which others have unwittingly left as a result of their ignorance. Thus contraception can, on occasion, be an aid to repopulation. Investigations carried out in the United States have even shown that the increase in the number of birth-control clinics had resulted in a considerable fall in the number of cases of voluntary sterilization. In the last century it used to be said that women instructed in the methods of dissociating pleasure and motherhood would take advantage of those methods to have no more children. The imaginations of the Puritans, excited by their own frustrations, showed them a bestial, selfish human race. They underestimated mankind's natural desire to perpetuate itself. They failed to realize that birth control can have lofty motives, can be linked with the desire to ensure a more harmonious life for the couple, and even more with the desire to give the children a better up-bringing.

A few months ago, spending a Sunday in Guadeloupe, I went to church in a little mountain village. Mass was celebrated by a priest with a pink face and a white beard. I went to see him afterwards in the sacristy. Having seen a lot of children in the church, I took the opportunity to ask the holy man what he thought about over-population in the West Indies. 'God will provide,' he told me. Every now and then our conversation was interrupted by parishioners coming to ask him to bless some object or other. I almost began to think I was in the presence of a magician. In the afternoon I went to see another priest who was younger, more cultivated, more modern. He spoke to me about a book which he had just read which vaunted the merits of 'reserved intercourse'. Would he have been so attracted if he had been acquainted with the detailed history of the Oneida community, founded in the last century in America? This was a strange, disquieting experiment, in which reserved intercourse was associated with both equality for women and a sort of matriarchy. This so-called 'reserve' was often a way for the woman to monopolize the orgasm for herself. Even when she too was deprived of it her frustration was not as great as the man's. Man regards sexual intercourse as a dramatic episode, comprising a development and a denouement, which admittedly must not be hurried, but which loses its attraction if it is extended indefinitely. Prolonged intimacy bores or annoys him. Woman, whose sexuality is more diffuse, is more easily satisfied with a passive exchange which involves the whole body rather than just the sexual organs. A motionless belly and electrified fingers: this is a fulfilment of which her partner is scarcely capable. Yet it seems that the masculine members of the Oneida community ended up by reaching such a climax. That is an achievement which, though perhaps less uncommon in the Far East, will always remain exceptional among the restless, highly strung peoples of the West. 'Petting' in America and 'marshing' in the Vendée are just vague approximations to it (which are sometimes enough to produce neurosis or impotence). Moreover, is there not an element of superstition in this avarice of sperm? The man's performance meets trickery on the part of the woman, and both of them fall into a rather unhealthy psychological affectation. As so often happens in these matters, the search for God leads to Satan.

I am not trying to amuse my readers with this account of my conversations in Guadeloupe. The first priest I talked to really looked as if he had come from the earthly paradise. The second was clumsily and honestly searching for the solution to a problem of whose gravity he had a certain inkling. Both of them, I think, were ignorant of the real strength of the Catholic position. It tends to keep sexual intercourse within the realm of sacred things. There the Church is on firm ground. It supports a fundamental instinct in woman, who seeks in motherhood the full physical use of her organs and the full moral use of her capacity for giving. It is also in keeping with that masculine sensibility which regards any diminution of the natural sexual act as a physiological sin. Sterility and *coitus interruptus* are mutilations: the Church is right to state this; neurologists are in full agreement. By accepting a risk of conception (which in any case is hard to eliminate completely) one invests the act of love with a responsibility which raises its value. Similarly, by observing periods of abstinence, one avoids the danger of saturation. The Catholic world maintains a certain tension between the sexes which somehow contributes to their pleasure.

A statistical finding which I read in Puerto Rico was extremely thought-provoking. In a clinic which supplied the 'pill', the women had been asked if, when they used it, the satisfaction they obtained from sexual intercourse had diminished or increased. Logically, there should have been a clear majority who obtained increased satisfaction—these volunteers of contraception, freed at last from the fears of motherhood, were able to give themselves up entirely to pleasure. In fact the answers were almost equally divided. Are we to assume that 'danger' is also a spice for pleasure? I shall refrain from any sort of generalization. Surveys of this sort have a very limited value. This one probably expressed only the reactions of a certain social group with certain traditions. All the same it is curious that the result should not have been more definite.[13]

Does the woman who thinks that she wants no more children know herself fully? Not always, since cases of regret have been recorded after voluntary sterilization. (A Chicago gynaecologist once told me of the bitter reproaches hurled at her by one of her patients, although the latter had been duly warned.) According to a paper read by Dr. Hans Lehfeldt to the conference of the Planned Parenthood Congress in New Delhi in 1959, certain failures in contraception must be attributed, not to imperfections in the methods, but to private hesitations on the part of the women using them. When I read this analysis I thought at first that it was merely a development of the Freudian cliché. But the experience of the clinics does in fact show that a certain number of women allow themselves to be checked by tiny difficulties. This is because their inner motivation is not very strong. They know that in the interests of their health or of their children they *ought* to limit their family, and they make a small effort in that direction 'to ease their consciences' (just as other women, who say they want to commit suicide, take an inadequate dose of barbiturate, to give death a slight chance of taking them). They ask doctors and social workers for a miracle-drug, an infallible contraceptive, and when they are told that none exists they lose heart and prefer to trust to luck, that great friend of women, that accomplice of their weakness. In reality they prefer Nature to go on working freely within them.[14]

In a way one might say that Catholics still await the arrival of a child as a happy surprise, something which upsets plans, disturbs the exaggerated neatness of modern life, an unsolicited gift from God to man. They accept 'family planning' only in vague forms. Protestants, on the other hand, regard family planning as virtuous. They consider that the prime object of marriage is the harmony of the couple, whereas Catholics consider this of secondary importance to a more essential aim, procreation. One might infer from this that physical love must be happier among the Protestants. But it is not enough to aim at happiness in order to attain it. In alcove as in church, the Calvinist atmosphere has something prosaic about it. The Catholic female, at once stricter and more animal-like, retains a special sex appeal of her own. By taking the risk of motherhood, she gives herself in a more absolute fashion. To eliminate that risk entirely is to devalue the body, to reduce it to the level of an article of food, to turn sexual enjoyment into a mere gastronomical pleasure. Such at least is the point of view of certain males, more interested in conquest than in satisfaction. (It is no accident that Don Juan was born in Seville.)

Sociologically, the Protestant attitude is gaining ground in the developed countries thanks to progress in employment and in the underdeveloped countries thanks to progress in education. In the first case birth control enables the women to satisfy their two fundamental desires by making a rational division between work and motherhood. In the second case it gives individuals that minimum of autonomy which enables their personalities to expand. The old Catholic natalism is even gradually becoming self-contradictory. All those 'surprise' children are preparing a uniform future for us. All those unique, irreplacable souls, if they were allowed to multiply indefinitely, would lead to the triumph of materialism.

Excessively strict prohibitions lead women to avoid their priests or lie to them. When the Church takes the question of birth control into politics she risks a severe defeat. In the last elections in Puerto Rico (a Catholic country) the new clerical party, which was sponsored by the bishops and campaigned against contraception, obtained only six per cent of the total votes. This is because public opinion was aware of certain ambiguities in the 'Roman' position. In recommending the rhythm method the Church claims to be respecting 'Nature'. But surely that method is rather a means of deceiving Nature? There is a continuous publicity campaign in the pious Press for the Ogino Calendar 'to tell you the fertile days'. The women who buy the calendar use it, of course, to find out the sterile days. Hygienic practices themselves comprise a good many subterfuges. A douche may be contraceptive or simply hygienic. The husband may be 'unaware' that his wife is wearing a diaphragm. The pill itself is ambivalent. 'If,' declared Pius XII on 12 September 1958, 'a woman takes this medicine, not with a view to preventing conception, but simply on medical advice, as a necessary remedy for a disease of the uterus or of the organism as a whole, she is producing an indirect sterilization, which is permitted in accordance with the general principle of dual-effect actions.' Similarly, as we have seen, it is possible to kill with a drug without sinning in the eyes of the Church, if one's aim is not to kill but to alleviate pain.

On the basis of this theory of the principal action, a Belgian canon has propounded a curious thesis: the temporary suppression of ovulation which the contraceptive pill produces artificially can, he says, occur naturally after childbirth. Cases of prolonged sterility in these conditions have been reported in India and the Congo. In reality these were perhaps not cases of sterility but of taboos; the whole question is anything but clear. Our canon none the less asserts that the spacing out of births is a 'normal' phenomenon, which primitive peoples have retained and civilized peoples have lost. Consequently, for the latter, 'during the months following childbirth, use of the pill is legitimate, for it only supports a natural mechanism which has accidentally become inadequate'.[15] Here we have an example of sheer Jesuitry. When people are too strict about principles they always end up by being too accommodating about exceptions.

The fact is, if the Church prefers the rhythm method, it is because this method forces the couples who use it to observe periods of continence when they must discipline their senses. The Ogino Calendar provides this discipline with precise rules. To observe these rules is to declare one's values. This is a lofty choice, but in order to have its full moral value it must be free. I once read an American book whose author tried to show that the practical behaviour of Catholics with regard to birth control was really not very different from that of Protestants. (In the United States this is often true—Catholic couples let their children come more easily at the beginning of their marriage, but later 'intervene' like the rest and often with methods forbidden by the Church.) But the same author observed that, according to a recent survey, use of the rhythm method is particularly widespread among Catholic *intellectuals*. It would therefore seem that a more thoughtful religious belief inspires a stricter discipline. This is a statistical finding which commands respect.[16] Let us hope that in the future the Catholic substitution of the word 'regulation' for the word 'control', a questionable verbal trick, will correspond less to a 'technical' fetishism than to a profound spiritual difference.

In time, and with scientific progress, it does not seem at all impossible that a wide measure of agreement could be established to regard as a sort of model a couple who, to begin with, employed the rhythm method (the arrival of children corresponding to their deliberate interruptions or to their mistakes) and used contraception at a later stage, after forming a normal family. That is a model which the Church does not yet dare recommend, but which many excellent Catholics already follow.

As for sexual intercourse outside marriage, it normally involves the use of contraception, which here offers a dual advantage: firstly it makes such intercourse more vigilant and reserves for married people sexual relations which are wholly free and natural; secondly it saves the woman from the terrible choice between abortion and an illegitimate child. For young girls the only satisfactory solution remains virginity. There exists a whole literature which maintains that this is 'bourgeois prejudice'. But a recent survey reveals that in France eighty per cent of the young people of all classes remain firmly attached to it. They are right, from the practical as well as the moral point of view. The 'pill' cannot (for reasons which we have mentioned) be given to minors, and the other methods are unreliable. Experts who want to guarantee 100 per cent safety are reduced to recommending a combination of two feminine contraceptives and one masculine contraceptive—one can scarcely see an adolescent girl initiating herself in life by means of lobster love-making. Virginity is therefore the contraceptive indicated in this case. The scientists attack it only in the name of a mistaken psychophysiology. At a gathering of *avant-garde* doctors I heard one of them ask: 'Which must we choose: frustration or pregnancy at fourteen?' Such is the havoc wreaked by psycho-analysis! Let us reply calmly that the terms of this comparison are not equal. Indeed the problem is invented (at least to a large extent) by being stated.

On this point, as on others, Catholic morality and scientific morality meet. As a general rule, only marriage can make well-balanced women and happy children. (In any case, as a free-thinker ingenuously remarked in the course of a recent investigation: 'So far we haven't found anything better.') To say that is not to formulate a principle but to state a fact. Unfortunately, whatever the principles are which are accepted and proclaimed, we shall always find ourselves faced with individual cases presenting special delicate problems. These too must be dealt with.

I admire the brave women who, in Britain as also in the United States (and for some time past in France), dare to take on responsibilities which other women avoid. I shall cite one example which has come to my notice. The laws of the State of New York say nothing either for or against sterilization. But many doctors are none the less afraid of trouble if their patients should later sue them. (In France, in a case of sterilization, a doctor could be sued for assault and battery.) So some ladies of goodwill intervene, open an office, and decide according to considerations of ordinary humanity whether or not to refer the women who consult them to a doctor willing to operate. This is at once very admirable and slightly disturbing.

Truth to tell, I have always felt a little uneasy among certain daughters of suffragettes, pioneers of free motherhood, who speak of large families in tones of disgust, consider man's sexual organ as a source of pleasure to be exploited, and set off, armed with a lawbook, a diaphragm, and a lipstick, to obtain conjugal power. They claim to be serving an ideal of conscious motherhood, a guarantee of the children's happiness. But the two terms have not been proved to be equivalent. Many children whose arrival was not wished for are finally loved as much as or more than the rest. Indeed the parents alter, upon their arrival, the theoretical idea they previously professed of the ideal size of the family. The ladies who run birth-control clinics have a fondness for rather subtle distinctions. They do not recommend the free use of contraceptive products without medical supervision, they do not want sterilization to be granted merely on request, and they prefer to communicate their secrets to the mothers of several children. All this is excellent, but there is something arbitrary about it. Where is the line drawn? Who is entitled to say: 'This is lawful, that is not'? These ladies arrogate this privilege to themselves. They secretly aspire to take the place of the priest and the parent, by settling spiritual problems in their stead, and of the doctor, by transferring to the social plane (where they are installed) questions which hitherto belonged to medicine. What we see here is in fact a struggle between rival groups of pedagogues. The pretensions of the ladies in the birth-control clinics are justified, in the first case, only if priests and parents show themselves to be incapable of giving the young the necessary sexual education, and in the second case only if the doctors take advantage of outdated legislature to avoid their normal responsibilities.

The Church is entitled to recommend certain practices. To exert pressure on the executive and the legislature is another matter. To try, as the American bishops recently did, to prevent the pagans of the Far East, who want to limit their populations, from receiving the necessary advice on this subject, is absurd. To claim the right to prohibit birth control for Protestants in countries with a large Catholic minority is already improper. As an American Catholic priest has remarked, it is a repetition of the mistake the Protestants made in temporarily imposing on the whole American population the prohibition of alcohol. Out of 2,200 doctors in Connecticut (where 46 per cent of the population are Catholic), 1,300 replied to a questionnaire on contraception, of whom 94 per cent showed hostility to the law forbidding it in that State. Yet it proved impossible to abrogate it. Out of fear of the Catholic vote, the Senators buried the proposals for revision of the law. One of the judges, to whom it was pointed out that contraceptive products were in fact to be found in the drugstores of Massachusetts, replied that 'perhaps the purchasers merely intended to collect them'. Faced with this general shirking of obligations, a certain Mrs. Giswold, following Margaret Sanger's example, decided to take action. She opened a clinic, read the birth announcements in the local papers, and wrote inviting the mothers to come and see her. She thus succeeded in provoking intervention on the part of the police, who came and closed her clinic. The case continues . . .

One cannot but approve of the efforts now being made by a few peace-makers to foster, on the one hand, a search for birth-control methods reconcilable with the Catholic rules, and, on the other hand, formulas for a provisional agreement making it possible to carry on the fight against overpopulation with due respect for philosophical and religious differences.

In the preceding pages I have tried to respect the complexity of the subject in analysing the different, sometimes contradictory, reactions which it arouses. In conclusion I should like to try to pick out the constants, which after all are the essential.

During the last few years people have concentrated too

exclusively on the study of contraceptive *methods*. The motivation behind contraception is more important. In the pre-industrial age, Swedish and then French peasants, the vast majority of them illiterate, started reducing their families without any knowledge of the mechanical or chemical methods which were used later on. More recently Japan has disciplined her birth-rate without benefit of pills. The task is more difficult in certain underdeveloped countries, for cultural or climatic reasons. But these countries enjoy advantages which the West has never known: Malthusian policies on the part of the governments (at least in South Asia) and technical progress in contraception.

Today a desire for family limitation is noticeable everywhere. The large family (over four children) is disappearing in the developed countries. One day it will be regarded as an insurance taken out in a period of high mortality, which the progress of hygiene has gradually made useless. A Shanghai doctor once said to me: 'All women want children, but none wants to have one every year.' I could have heard this remark anywhere in the world. Whether they are Communists or capitalists, mothers voluntarily use only about a third of their reproductive potential (three children instead of nine).[17]

Everywhere, reproduction is a play with four characters: the Man, who wants to assert his virility without suffering all the consequences; the Woman, who at one and the same time wants to give herself, perpetuate herself, and preserve herself; the Child, a future character whose right to happiness is gradually being recognized; and the State, which, now calling for future soldiers and future taxpayers, now dreading the prospect of having to support future unemployed, proudly distributes family allowances with its right hand and discreetly issues contraceptives with its left. All four have—or ought to have—two enemies in common: overpopulation marked by famine or degradation, and secret abortion.

On this last point a certain contrast seems to be appearing at present between the East and the West. The laws of the Communist countries authorize abortion in certain 'social' circumstances, which are usually generously interpreted. Three tendencies can be distinguished in the official mind, which modify one another. One, egalitarian and dictatorial, shows a certain complaisance towards abortion, because it can be controlled, more easily than contraception, by the State which grants or refuses it according to social criteria. A second tendency, rationalistic in character, regards abortion as a waste (useless beginning of pregnancy, wasted hours, medical expenses) which an efficient society should avoid. A third, emancipatory, tendency aims at protecting women's freedom and health. In practice this last tendency serves as an alibi, making it possible to rectify the doctrinaire natalism of official Marxism. The conditions required for legal abortion vary slightly from one country to another. In Czechoslovakia the applicant is asked to state her age, how many children she has, and her social position. In Poland a certificate given by a doctor is sufficient. In Hungary medical authorization is a matter of form: the applicant has only to insist to obtain satisfaction. Only East Germany interprets her legislation in a restrictive sense (probably in an attempt to remedy by a maximum birth-rate the continuous exodus of her population).

These laws, put into practice during the last few years, have naturally resulted in a considerable increase in legal abortions: in Czechoslovakia they rose from 7,000 to 61,000 in 1957–8, in Poland from 44,000 to 79,000 in 1958–9. One might logically expect a parallel reduction in the number of secret abortions. But this has fallen only slightly in Czechoslovakia and has remained constant in Poland. The number of births has none the less *increased.* How are we to reconcile these data? The legalization of 'social' abortion has led to increased hospitalization of secret abortions; as a result, a very large proportion of these have been included in the official statistics. There are no grounds for deducing from this that the overall number of abortions has risen, and there is no doubt that they have become less dangerous. Moreover, the minimum period which must elapse between an abortion and a birth is much shorter than that which separates one birth from another. The general effect of these various factors is an increase in all the figures: the number of legal abortions, the number of secret abortions, and the total number of births and abortions.

According to Dr. Tietze, an American doctor who has made a special study of these experiments in Eastern Europe, therapeutic abortion practised in these conditions presents fewer risks than childbirth. In Hungary and Czechoslovakia in particular it only rarely has fatal consequences. The statistics of these two countries are much more satisfactory in this respect than those of the Scandinavian countries. This is probably because in Hungary and Czechoslovakia abortion is authorized only during the first three months of pregnancy. Perhaps something should be said here of a certain 'humanization' of abortion.

In Western Europe there is much greater awareness of the dangers of the operation, particularly of the sterility which it may cause. Natalists and Malthusians even exaggerate these consequences, the former to encourage women to go on to normal childbirth, the latter to encourage them to use contraceptives. Treating every abortion as a crime, without making a distinction, essential though it is, between the limited risks of therapeutic abortion and the much more serious risks of secret abortion, is held to be 'showing respect for life'. Admittedly the origin of life is to be seen in conception. It is impossible to make a scientifically valid distinction at a subsequent point in time. The natural conscience has none the less always considered that life develops *progressively*. During the first few days a mother feels herself the owner of her child. Many ask themselves aloud when at the doctor's: 'What am I going to do with *it*? I don't know if I'm going to keep it.' And if the doctor sermonizes they calmly reply: 'But it's only a fortnight old!' Sometimes an attempt is made to find some compromise between the absolutes of science and morality and the relatives of human sensibility. In France a therapeutic abortion can be obtained only if the mother's 'life' is in danger, and, in order to establish the existence of this danger, certificates are required from three doctors, including one forensic expert—a process which is so long that it risks being completed too late and is therefore scarcely ever used. In Switzerland the opinion of two doctors and the existence of 'a serious and permanent threat to health' are sufficient.[18]

Everywhere the selfish young woman who wants to avoid motherhood entirely is the object of disapproval. Even in the most 'advanced' Communist countries she is confronted with a certain formal moral resistance. On the other hand, the mother of three or more children who asks to resign from her position as a breeder, or at least to have a period of rest, is considered worthy of interest. Even in the most reactionary countries, the authorities move easily from total prohibition of any kind of antinatalist practice, to acceptance of certain 'medical' and then 'social' circumstances. (In really overpopulated countries, such as Japan in the early post-war period, the two types of circumstances coincide in many cases, the poverty being such as to exercise a definite influence on health.) Certain subtle attitudes borrow from two opposite systems. They accept, for instance, contraception, but balance this with financial inducements to childbirth, and even sometimes a certain amount of natalist propaganda. Where sterilization is authorized it is generally practised on the occasion of a delivery. The woman who goes into hospital to have her last baby comes out with her Fallopian tubes ligatured. In the final analysis mothers of large families and sterilized women, instead of being in opposition, form a single group.

All these methods are expressions of an attempt to reconcile the reproduction of the species and the fulfilment of individuals. Between one country and another practices differ according to the national traditions, the degree of education, and the urgency of the problem. When an extremely rapid fall in the birth-rate seems indispensable (as was the case in Japan in 1948) abortion is made easy; it is an unpleasant method, but it enables rapid results to be obtained. Once the fall has started, the attention which had been concentrated on this end is transferred to the means; an endeavour is made to replace abortion by preventive control. This adjustment takes a certain time. The number of abortions may even increase to begin with, for they occur to make good the failures of inexperienced contraception. This is what happened in Japan, but only up to 1956. In the long run the combined efforts of the State and the doctors, falling in with the families' obvious interests, are bound to triumph. According to Riallin, a study of the Japanese statistics shows already that, while women often resort to contraception after the unpleasant experience of an abortion, 'few give up contraceptive methods in order to resort to abortion'.

In India, another country with an acute population problem where the authorities tried to move more delicately at first, almost complete failure was the result. Consequently their methods are being revised. In the third Indian plan 250 million rupees, that is to say five times more than in the two previous plans put together, are earmarked for the fight against overpopulation. The Federal Government has decided to follow the example set by several Indian states in subsidizing voluntary sterilization.[19] (Several hundred thousand people have already been sterilized since 1956.) But this effort still seems to be inadequate. An official committee recently called for more energetic measures, going as far as the legalization of abortion, a national campaign in favour of sterilization, the large-scale production and distribution of contraceptives, and even a system of progressive taxation of families with more than four children, all this under the supervision of a 'Minister for the Control of the Population'. It is a matter for regret that action of this sort has to be considered. But if the developed countries can dispense with it, that is because they have resorted since the nineteenth century to more discreet methods of control. The germinal river having been disciplined in time, before the great floods, we have no need to build emergency dykes in a hurry. The difference is in *tempo*, not in direction.

After diverging for a long time men have begun to come together.[20] Yesterday magic was already, in some of its aspects, an uncertain form of science. Today the longing for knowledge and dignity is spreading throughout the world. The desire to limit one's progeny in order to allow it to develop is perhaps the greatest of modern progressive forces. Those bigots who denounce it are fighting, in the name of charity, against a very lofty form of charity. To identify the operation of the mechanisms of Nature with a divine will is to refuse to see the progress which man has made in trying to limit their scope. If a divine plan exists these efforts and this progress necessarily form part of it. They are, according to Christian doctrine, the efforts and the progress of a man whom God created in His likeness.

Six

A FEW GUIDING RULES

AFTER dealing with subjects so intimately concerned with the life, happiness, and dignity of man it would be unforgivable not to conclude by trying to be *useful*. I shall therefore try to formulate a few guiding rules.

Let us begin with what is most urgent. Three milliard human beings are on their way towards life. We can and must try to stem this flood. But some of the invaders are virtually with us already; we cannot prevent them from arriving. We shall therefore have to feed them. Hunger, a vague and terrifying subject, lends itself to a great many dogmatic statements. Josué de Castro declares: 'Nearly two-thirds of mankind are suffering from hunger.' But Colin Clark replies: 'At the most ten per cent.' This example shows what divergencies the subject permits. In order to know what a population really consumes in one year, complicated and hazardous calculations have to be made about the losses suffered between harvesting and consumption, the use of food for animals, etc. A ration may be at once inadequate in proteins, vitamins, and mineral elements and adequate in calories. Moreover, it is difficult to calculate the value of every food in calories. It is even more difficult to determine the psychophysiological threshold of *actual* hunger. Needs vary according to climate. (Fortunately the over-populated regions are generally also hot regions where it is possible to eat less.) Malnutrition is more common than under-feeding, and it is often due to the bad habits of the people concerned.

Whole populations destroy, in the preparation of their pap, the vitamins they need. (Consequently it is not so much a question of feeding them as of teaching them how to feed themselves.) Nor should we confuse chronic hunger with the annual period of hunger preceding the harvest, which has been a part of peasant life for thousands of years and which the civilized peoples of today perpetuate in Lent and Ramadan. This annual hunger has no serious consequences. It is even possible, as certain specialists assert, that it sets in motion a process of adjustment which is beneficial to health.

The demagogues of hunger ignore these distinctions. They have drawn up a list of forty elements which they regard as necessary to the maintenance of health. In their eyes a man who, although he does not regularly absorb these forty elements, declares that he feels perfectly well and refuses to die, is in the wrong, just as Molière's Argan was in the wrong in Monsieur Purgon's eyes. He is forcibly enrolled in the army of the victims of capitalism. For in the last analysis it is a question of drawing up an indictment of the capitalist system. Josué de Castro writes: 'Mankind is divided today into the under-fed and the well-fed. The latter must feed the former, otherwise the starving two-thirds of mankind will rise in revolt against the well-fed third.' To read these words one might imagine that the solution of the problem depends simply on the generosity of the West. In private Josué de Castro is even more precise: his words are addressed to the Americans. But if it is a question of apportioning responsibility, mention should also be made of that of the U.S.S.R. (which refuses to join in world aid projects, excludes foreign workers, and makes sure that she has no surpluses to distribute), that of China (which sacrifices lives rather than admit her errors by asking for help), and that of the under-developed countries (which often fail to help themselves). To simplify the problem and name scapegoats is to encourage violence and jeopardize possibilities of co-operation.

This demagogy is not only sometimes dangerous, but, more often than not, futile. It is extremely difficult for a Westerner to imagine the dream world in which an underfed Southern Asiatic lives. We claim to share his suffering by means of our sympathy. But there is an element of misunderstanding in all this. If we really succeeded in making contact, we should discover in him a slightly contemptuous indifference towards us. In helping him, we should like to postpone his death. But nowadays, in a sense, he does not die at all, because he has no clear awareness of his individuality and because his religion tells him that life is an illusion. We Westerners know that after a hundred years at the most our contours will disappear, and this idea makes us feel uncomfortable in advance. The Hindu, already installed in the stream of metamorphoses, does not experience this dread. How can a liberation of that sort be compared with the satisfaction we derive from our activities, our standard of living, our hopes of longevity? There is no single scale in which to weigh such disparate ideals. The sphere of religion would have to be separated from that of food, and in practice this is very difficult, for to a large extent they correspond. The Hindu would often rather respect certain taboos than eat normally. A curious element of *amour-propre* also enters into it. 'If you gave us your ration,' a Hindu once said to me disgustedly, 'we wouldn't even be able to digest it.' If we are to take immediate action we must be aware of this resistance. Indeed perhaps it is our duty not to shake this resignation unduly before we can guarantee satisfaction. In the long run, however, archaic mental attitudes are doomed. All the populations in the world are going to enter the international economy one after another. How can we help them to do so?

The instinctive reaction of the man of goodwill is to apply the principle of communicating vessels. L. Tabah, after dividing the world into two regions whose average incomes he estimates at 100 dollars for the inhabitants of one and 1,000 dollars for the inhabitants of the other, urges the latter to agree to the sacrifices needed to enable the former to double their income in thirty-five years. The donators would make an increasing contribution starting at 4·4 per cent (of their income) and going up to 13·2 per cent—instead of ·4 per cent as at present. At the end of the process the West would therefore be giving thirty-three times more than it gives now. This would be a severe imposition, but the target would not be reached. For this sort of proposal neglects the difficulties arising from the limited capacity for absorption of the countries in question, from the need to avoid competition in production between them, and from the structure of the existing international monetary system. Let us try to situate the trouble in order to find effective remedies.

From 1950 to 1957, while the average individual income in the developed countries rose by twenty dollars, that in the underdeveloped countries rose by only one dollar. Trade between the developed countries increased in spectacular fashion, but the exports of the underdeveloped countries increased only slowly. Even so, these exports represent eight times the volume of the gifts they receive, so that slight fluctuations in their value are sufficient to nullify international aid. To put an end to this paradox, various systems have been proposed. Raising prices artificially has the drawback of stimulating an already excessive production. The surpluses, even if they are kept off the market, exercise an influence, for they accumulate and remain on the producers' hands, a situation which eventually leads the State concerned to demand a revision of the agreement. It would seem preferable to regularize the producers' *receipts* by means of compensatory mechanisms (the opening of credits or increased aid in the form of food in the event of a fall). This is the gist of a recent American proposal. The developed countries should also try to increase their own consumption of certain products of the underdeveloped countries (coffee or cocoa) by freeing them from taxation.

Projects for world aid have so far met with resistance by a powerful negative coalition: Americans unwilling to allow their dollars to be distributed by Communists, Russians reluctant to join in any common action with capitalists, Britons secretly hostile to a rise in the value of certain basic products which they import. Western loans have for a long time been subject to profitability tests which the underdeveloped countries could not satisfy. Even today one still occasionally hears 'liberals' suggesting 'throwing the animal into the water to teach it to swim'. This is political murder or suicide: the victim either drowns or calls other rescuers (Communists) to his aid.

The developed countries can no longer decently use against the underdeveloped countries rules of economic liberalism which they no longer observe in their own economies. In the developed countries agriculture is gradually being caught up in the rising movement of industry. (The frontier between the two sectors is even becoming rather vague—pig-breeding and poultry-breeding no longer belong, properly speaking, to country life.) But as food consumption remains limited there is increasing agricultural over-production. To dispose of the surplus, governments are led to subsidize agricultural exports to other solvent countries, thus financing their own industrial rivals. Speaking for France, Wilfrid Baumgartner has proposed establishing a different system, which would transfer the benefit of these subsidies to the underdeveloped countries. This is an excellent suggestion. Unfortunately, as a result of old habits, rich exporters and poor consumers are not always complementary.

In spite of the rapid decrease in the rural population, American agricultural production increased by an average of 2·5 per cent per annum during the last ten years, while the population increased by only 1·7 per cent. Even in Europe people are beginning to talk of 'an obsession with growth' and 'agricultural overproduction'. But the excesses of some do not correspond to the deficiencies of the others, and moreover are not suited to them. A mutual adjustment is necessary. The West must look for ways of linking its system with that of the underdeveloped countries in such a way as to spare them the superhuman efforts which an isolated attempt at emancipation would impose on them. Tomorrow the surplus skilled workers which the United States will produce will be able to find work and spiritual satisfaction in helping in the emancipation of the less advanced countries. The hunger of one group and the neurasthenia of the other can thus be appeased together, *if the problem remains contained within certain limits*. This is a fundamental condition.

Already a new aid strategy is taking shape, which consists of using food as a means of fighting inflation in the country receiving assistance, within the context of an overall plan comprising not only agricultural but also industrial development measures and human investments. A fund of 100 million dollars is going to be used in this spirit for three years under the auspices of the 'Food for Peace Program'. This sum still represents only one per cent of the bilateral aid given by the United States. It is impossible to obtain a satisfactory solution either by this world-wide effort (which is under the control of a hundred states) or by bilateral aid (which is all too often governed by the size of the national surpluses of the developed countries, and therefore irregular and open to description as 'colonialist'). It is up to the developed countries to agree in the course of the coming years on a programme of common aid in the general interest.

George Ball, the American Under-Secretary of State, has suggested that these countries should devote one per cent of their national incomes to this task. His suggestion bears witness to an interesting evolution in public opinion, but it has no great value in itself. The percentage suggested may even be regarded as something of a joke, for it is lower than the contribution to which France at present agrees. Moreover, an approach of this sort is dangerous, for the underdeveloped countries, in a majority at the United Nations, could later demand successive increases in the percentage, much as in the internal politics of the Western countries the 'advanced' parties have demanded and obtained increases in what was at first a very moderate income tax. The existing society of nations would not survive this sort of demagogy.

The choice lies in fact between two alternatives. Either the West wants to keep its special character, its civilization, and in that case there is a limit to the aid it can give. Or it agrees to lose its identity in a world shaped entirely by the necessities of overpopulation. Let us try to imagine the consequences of such a fusion. In North America, less than a tenth of the cereals produced is destined for human consumption. The rest feeds human beings only at one remove: in the shape of meat, eggs, poultry. In the underdeveloped countries, on the other hand, almost the entire cereal yield is directly consumed by human beings, which, from the calories point of view, is a far better state of affairs. If the world food shortage were to deteriorate seriously the West could (theoretically) adopt this practice. The result would be a permanent fast for New York, London, and Paris, and a shortage of proteins (and hence of energy) for mankind as a whole. But the world would have succeeded in increasing the number of 'half-lives'.

In all probability this renunciation of meat would have been preceded by a renunciation of the motor car and of a great many other material advantages of civilization. And finally, after sacrificing comforts or luxuries, we should throw moral values to the winds. The citizens of the overpopulated world would behave like the occupants of a besieged fortress, in which, seeing that everybody must work for the common defence, not only do pleasures become out of place, but any kind of disinterested activity is a sort of treason.

I cannot believe that the West will agree to this degradation.[21] Let us return then to the search for truly practicable methods of co-operation. The first duty of the developed countries is to put themselves in a position to give effective help to their less fortunate partners by reforming the international monetary system now in force. During the last few years, the aid, inadequate though it was, given by the Anglo-Saxon countries, was sufficient to produce in those countries crises in the balance of payments, worsened by speculation, which led to restrictions in exchange and production. Palliatives were found for these crises, but not remedies. Gold remains theoretically the basis of the currencies of the free world. We no longer accept the logical consequences of this principle, but we do not dare to abandon it either. This contradiction will not continue indefinitely. It is up to the experts to examine the problem without delay, and up to the statesmen to set about solving it instead of devoting the greater part of their energies to outdated rivalry in matters of prestige. The world's progress depends above all today on the ability of the great enlightened powers (the United States, Europe, and, I hope, the U.S.S.R.) to concert their action.

This action cannot be confined to the granting of gifts or credits. Calculations made in this respect, even using exceptionally optimistic hypotheses, indicate only tiny increases in *per capita* income. Technical assistance is probably more important. But technical assistance assumes the actual or potential existence of local personnel capable of receiving it. Help can really be given only to those who put themselves in a position to be helped. In order to take this step, certain backward countries will have to use authoritarian methods. This does not necessarily imply that they are going to fall into the power of Moscow or Peking, and will not be able to become more liberal at a later stage in their development. The West will have all the more reason to count on this liberalization in that it will have helped them to achieve their break-through, first by giving them financial and technical aid, and then (when these countries have reached the industrial stage) by admitting their products into a sector of the world's work. But it is important to realize that success will necessarily be slow to come.

It is, in fact, a question of handling economic entities characterized by inadequate energy, a dense population, and men of mediocre physiological and intellectual quality. It is difficult to industrialize rapidly in these conditions. It would indeed seem wiser to give priority to programmes of agricultural modernization. Even then, there are grave risks of disappointment. The failure of the 'development communities' (created under the aegis of the United Nations in certain underdeveloped countries to mobilize on a voluntary basis their latent productive forces) is proof of this.

In October 1952, on the anniversary of Gandhi's birth, Pandit Nehru solemnly inaugurated one of these communities, as if it were a historic event. Chester Bowles, the United States Ambassador, attended the ceremony; shortly afterwards he presented a contribution from his government, and even helped in the digging of some irrigation canals. In a book published in 1956 he still hoped for miraculous results. 'Millions of young men and old are going to give a few hours a day to their villages and their country after their own work is over. . . . I can already imagine a wave of building which will sweep across 500,000 villages and change the face of the entire sub-continent.' What wonderful American simplicity! What is the position today?

The overall report prepared by the United Nations secretariat in 1960 is extremely reserved. It notes that the projects of general interest are more often than not misunderstood by the villagers. They do not use the latrines, they allow the wells to be contaminated. In Malaysia as in India, the adults show little desire to learn to read. The amount of work provided for community tasks is very small: sometimes one or two days a year. Paradoxically, it is chiefly *projects* which are lacking. A road seems an abstract idea to peasants absorbed in the little problems of their village. They do not understand the meaning of co-operation, and refuse to share in work which will chiefly profit somebody else. Agrarian reforms which have been decided on are applied only slowly and imperfectly. Spending[22] proves more attractive than saving. It has been impossible to record any appreciable development of village industry. Government aid is accepted as a bounty, and evokes no response from the population. The authors of the report conclude by advocating recourse to a certain degree of 'democratic' compulsion. Local governments should have the right to levy taxes payable in labour. This is already a step in the direction of the Chinese solution, the drawbacks of which I mentioned earlier.

'Progressive' authors write as if it were sufficient to suppress liberty in order to create prosperity. Nothing could be further from the truth. In the West, on the contrary, liberty and prosperity are linked together and this combination holds a special appeal for the nationals of the Communist world, as we have seen in recent years at the gates to West Berlin and Hong Kong. Liberty everywhere retains a concrete meaning, for nobody likes to be torn away from his environment and his natural vocation on the pretext of social duty. Even the poorest of men can still *lose* an environment, habits, a little home, a congenial job. Governments which take these last refuges away from the poor without being able to promise them a definite improvement in their lot are condemning themselves to meeting strong passive resistance.

In present conditions the underdeveloped countries seem destined to oscillate for a long time between anarchy and tyranny, without making much progress towards their target. But birth control offers the possibility of a short cut.

This problem of birth control also arises in the developed countries of Europe and has been treated there in very different ways, as we shall see from a study of two inversely typical countries: Sweden and France.

Many Westerners, irritated by descriptions of a society of incredible perfection, picture Sweden as a prey to depravity, destined for depopulation, and ravaged by neurasthenia. What is the truth?

Birth control was not originally the effect of a governmental decision in this country any more than it was in any other European country. It expressed the spontaneous reaction of a population against the fall in its standard of living. Contraception developed first of all among the poor, even in the country. (If they still have rather more children than the well-to-do that is chiefly due to the isolation of certain areas, where medical influence scarcely penetrates.) Moreover the fall in the birth-rate is not due simply to contraception, but also to the fairly late average age of marriage (twenty-five for women, twenty-seven for men).

Even today Sweden has no definite demographic policy. She was indeed concerned for some time about her population's stagnation. From 1910 to 1938 a law forbade the sale of contraceptive products. This ban has been lifted. A law of 1946 even compels chemists' shops to sell contraceptives and plans are being made to put vending machines into service. However, the traditional contraceptive methods are still those most used. Swedish law authorizes sterilization or abortion in certain fixed circumstances. In fact, sterilization is hardly ever practised except on parents suffering from syphilis, alcoholism, or serious hereditary diseases, and legal abortion is allowed only on a recommendation by two doctors to the Ministry of Health, with whom the final decision lies. Abuses are therefore very rare: in 1960 there were only 3,000 legal abortions compared to over 100,000 births, whereas in Hungary the first figure exceeds the second. Naturally the official Swedish figure has to be completed by the number of secret abortions, of which estimates vary between 10,000 and 20,000 a year. If we accept that the real figure falls inside this range we have to conclude that the development of contraception has made it possible to reduce the number of deliberate 'accidents' to less than one-fifth of the number of births. This is a result which the natalist countries that denounce abortion in violent terms are a long way from reaching.

The Swedes' birth-rate is low, but so is their mortality. (Their infant mortality is indeed the lowest in the world.) Their expectation of life is sixty-seven for men, seventy for women. These figures testify to the achievement of the pattern of life which was aimed at: a child wanted by its parents, surviving the dangers of birth, and guaranteed seven decades of a full life. Nor does the birth-rate, as is often thought, describe a constantly falling curve. From 1935–9 to 1945–9, the birth-rate rose from 14 to 19 per 1,000. Sweden therefore followed the movement which occurred during the same period in France, England, and the United States. Properly speaking, the Swedish attitude is not so much Malthusian as liberal. This country without prejudices instituted sex education, treats mental defectives as sick people rather than delinquents, allows artificial insemination, etc.

There are a few shadows on the picture, however. Sweden has not felt able to take her policy the whole way. She does not allow girls under eighteen to take advantage of the contraceptive facilities which she grants their elders. These adolescent girls are none the less influenced by the general atmosphere of sexual freedom which reigns in the country, and therefore exposed to risks. To refuse them access to contraceptive products is to condemn them to abortion. Even if the total number of abortion cases is small it is disturbing to note that a considerable proportion of them are teenagers. In Denmark, where the same problem exists, people are beginning to advocate the two practical remedies for which the logic of the system calls: an extension of legal abortion, or the introduction of contraceptive propaganda into sex education.

Sweden has a high suicide-rate. Some commentators connect this phenomenon with neuroses set up by an overdeveloped social organization or with a general lack of vigour due to inadequate demographic pressure. It is difficult to separate these social factors from such natural factors as long winter nights, isolation, etc. We might note, however, that nearby Norway, subject to the same natural conditions but more puritanical in character, has a far lower suicide-rate. When the Swedes are reproached for their loose morals they reply: 'We are not more depraved than other people, but just less hypocritical. What is hidden in other countries takes place in broad daylight in Sweden. This is less unhealthy.' Their reasoning is attractive, but certain individual disasters are calculated to awaken a new appreciation, if not of hypocrisy, at least of modesty. Divorces and suicides can be compared to red lights whose growing brightness deserves to arouse attention. No doubt the conclusion we should draw is that a country where contraception is allowed has all the more need of a certain moral discipline.

In France a law of 31 July 1920 prohibits under pain of imprisonment and fines not only the sale of contraceptives but even the divulging of contraceptive methods. This law was passed by surprise during a morning sitting which was supposed to be devoted to discussion of a law of amnesty, without the Health Committee being asked to give its opinion beforehand. Some wits asked whether there were plans to prosecute the authors of obstetrical treatises, the publishers of Madame de Sévigné's *Letters*, and the Catholic Church itself (since that Church encourages people to pronounce the vow of chastity). Lhopiteau, the Minister of Justice, replied: 'We shall revise the law later if need be, but pass it now.' This law, which was passed in the hope of making good the terrible human losses of the First World War, had no effect on the French birth-rate. This went on falling from 1922 to 1935. During the whole of this period the number of abortions remained considerable and the number of convictions minimal.

In 1933 I interviewed Dr. Thierry de Martel, a famous and highly respected surgeon, on this subject. He told me: 'The woman who wants an abortion always manages to obtain one, in one way or another. Several times women have come to ask me to operate on them. I refused. Among those women there were some whom I saw again shortly afterwards, in my surgery or in hospital, suffering from salpingitis, and sometimes dying, as the result of an illegal abortion'. He had in fact repeated Margaret Sanger's crucial experience. Martel added: 'There are very few women who systematically terminate their pregnancies. Most of them don't want to be pregnant at certain times, in certain circumstances. . . . Take the example of a young girl who, for fear of the scandal and the possible consequences for the rest of her life, wants to avoid having a child. It is extremely probable that later on that same young girl, having married, will on the contrary want to have a child. But she will be unable to, because an abortion carried out in unfavourable conditions will have made her sterile. Obviously there is something shocking about this situation. It seems to me that the law as it stands does not ensure a rise in the birth-rate. On the other hand, as there is no legal alternative to secret abortion, this is extremely common and results in therapeutic accidents which lower the number of subsequent births. The use of birth control might therefore eventually lead not to a fall but to a rise in the birth-rate.'[23] All this remains true today. Taking up the subject again after thirty years, I realize how slow human progress can be.

French doctors go on piously reciting their professional code: 'The doctor must be very solicitous of human life. He must carefully refrain, except when it is therapeutically necessary, from any action which might jeopardize it or prevent its reproduction.' It is true that the phrase 'therapeutically necessary' can cover a great many measures. In this respect some doctors are more accommodating than others, but the latter, out of fear of losing their patients, are all the more strict towards their easy-going colleagues. When they are urged to consider the practical consequences of their attitude, they reply: 'It is up to the State to shoulder its responsibilities!' But this the State will not do. Consequently a woman intimidated by the law and rejected by the doctor goes to an abortionist, or else wages a horrible war upon herself with pins or pieces of glass. In the end the result is that one life has been suppressed, another has been jeopardized, a woman has been made sterile, a future has been sacrificed—but our Pharisees consider that their hands are clean. The legislator authorized nothing, the doctor advised nothing, the State knew nothing: everybody is innocent.

Nobody nowadays defends the 1920 law any more. Its loopholes are known to everybody. From the start, the sale of contraceptives for men has been authorized, because they are also preservatives against venereal disease. Without any publicity their sales increase every year by an average of twenty per cent (twenty million units in 1960). But the sale of most contraceptives for women remains illegal. However, there are doctors who will prescribe them all the same (for health reasons) for their patients, who then merely have the trouble of having them brought into France through the fairly loose net of the Customs.[24] The French Medical Council officially permits its members to prescribe occasionally 'natural' methods of birth control. Finally, the Public Prosecutor's department has in practice stopped treating abortion as a criminal offence.

A project for a new law was tabled by the French Socialist group on 28 April 1961. Here is the text of Article 2: 'Permission is given for the sale by pharmaceutical chemists of such products and objects calculated to prevent pregnancy as shall be listed in official regulations: these regulations shall list those products and objects which are not to be furnished by chemists except on a medical prescription.' Other parliamentary deputies go further and advocate complete freedom. But as yet there does not seem to be a majority in favour of any positive solution. Pending such a solution, we must content ourselves with this compromise: the failure to enforce the law as it stands. Contraceptive clinics were opened in 1961, in Grenoble and then in Paris, without giving rise to police action. However, the French Medical Council called on those of its members who were connected with these clinics to terminate this connection on pain of being eventually struck off the Register.[25] Some of the doctors in question allowed themselves to be intimidated. Others decided to take action against the Medical Council before the Council of State. Thus, little by little, the debate is warming up. Unfortunately it is complicated by rather sordid professional rivalries. The orthodox doctors accuse the innovators of 'touting for patients', while the innovators, having formed themselves into a society, take cover behind the 1901 Law on Associations. (They practise birth control, but among themselves.) However, is not the opening of a clinic an act of propaganda in itself? To decide this question, the law is being examined in detail. Particular attention is being given to a judgement of the Supreme Court of Appeal settling the case of a lady herborist who had sold 'clowns' caps and mignonette sponges'. She was convicted because she had sold 'a *considerable* number of objects'. How many 'mignonettes' must one sell to become guilty? Pettiness of this sort scarcely redounds to the honour of France. Let us hope that the legislature will decide to tackle the problem boldly.

I do not pretend to tell it where its duty lies, but perhaps I may make a few observations calculated to enlighten it. In my opinion the subject concerns contrary philosophical or religious attitudes between which it is no part of the State's duty to decide. The State's function is to preserve the nation's vitality, to watch over the protection of public health, and to ensure that the public is accurately informed. I shall deal briefly with these three points.

It is often stated that since a certain number of births are not wanted, the birth-rate will fall if contraception becomes easier and better known. The problem has to be seen as a whole. The spread of birth control is bound up with the fight against sterility and against abortion.[26] Its effect is therefore not exclusively Malthusian. Whereas France has just opened her first birth-control clinic, England is celebrating the fortieth anniversary of hers. Yet from 1955 to 1959 the annual number of births increased by 91,000 in England and by only 24,000 in France, for a population of roughly equal size. Why should it be assumed that the French are particularly selfish or that they love children less than other peoples? This sort of defeatism has to be eliminated as others have been. The once widely current image of the miserly, protectionist, stay-at-home Frenchman has already been discarded. The same treatment should be given to the myth according to which the French would be incapable of maintaining the birth-rate which they share with the Germans, the English, and the Dutch, if, like their neighbours, they knew that contraceptives existed and could eventually buy them.

The legislature's action would not necessarily be in only one direction. If, against all probability, the repeal of the 1920 law leads to a considerable and inopportune fall in the birth-rate, that fall could be remedied by appropriate measures. Obviously the State could never regulate the birth-rate with the same precision as the Bank regulates the volume of monetary circulation by varying the bank rate. Yet we have seen since 1939 that measures of encouragement to the family could be effective, whereas directly anti-Malthusian measures were not. Another rise of the same sort—and one which would not necessarily be burdensome—seems a possibility in the future. The results obtained in that way would indeed be much more imposing than those which are expected today from the maintenance of an ignorance doomed to be dispelled sooner or later by the progress of education and communications.

Protect health? That means supervising or prohibiting products whose effects are uncertain as yet, such as the contraceptive pills. Other countries have been bolder in this respect. It seems to me that France ought to take advantage of her tardiness to learn from the experiments which those other countries have made and will go on making.

Make sure that the public is accurately informed? That means giving all the young (we shall have to come to that in the end) an objective, carefully graded, sex education. They would then stop imagining that there are such things as perfect contraceptives which can be used without medical supervision, and would know that the rhythm method gives satisfactory results only if it is very strictly observed.

A country helps to define itself by choosing its policy on sex. As a Frenchman with no party ties, I hope that in this respect France may prove herself worthy of the idea I have formed of her from observation of her élites: a liberal nation with an enlightened Catholicism.

France is fortunate in no longer having any demographic problem to solve on her territory. In leaving Algeria, she freed herself from the one she had created there by taking progress across the Mediterranean. She no longer has any direct contact with overpopulation except in the West Indies. But it is still incumbent on her to set the example at home of a fully harmonious society, and she will have to adopt a definite position at the United Nations in the debates occasioned by world overpopulation. These two problems are separate and have to be treated differently, but France's principles must not be contradictory.

One often hears it said that the American government would like to make its aid to underdeveloped countries conditional on their adoption of contraception. How can a legend of that sort have come into existence? On this subject there have been a cautious statement by John D. Rockefeller and a rather curt declaration by Black, the Director of the World Bank. There has also been a certain amount of discreet and diffuse activity by foundations which have links with both American industry and certain underdeveloped countries in Asia. It is only in this way that a certain (very limited) 'Malthusian' assistance is given. But even those Americans who advocate more open intervention confine themselves to noting that in fact, in certain countries, the United States have financed increases in population rather than improvements in the standard of living. They would like to be able to tell the peoples concerned: 'You are free to continue on these lines, but there are better things to do and if you are willing to try, we will help you.' Here we are a long way from the 'genocide' about which people talk.

Moreover the activity of the American government is not aimed in that direction. President Eisenhower and President Kennedy both adopted a contrary position in the course of the last presidential election. The present administration does not even take any account of the alarming reports sent in by its experts. It certainly does not envisage suggesting birth control to countries who would not want it. Indeed—in compliance with a majority decision taken by the United Nations in 1961—it refuses to entertain the idea of granting aid to those who would wish to receive it (the countries of South Asia). Whenever the problem comes before the Assembly at New York the Scandinavians are the only Western countries who support the Malthusian cause. The South American delegates fulminate and their opposition intimidates most of their colleagues.[27] The European Latins stand together. Britain does not dare to intervene. The World Health Organization itself is hostile. When a resolution is discussed which touches vaguely on the subject, every word is closely examined to make certain that nothing is said. In New York a United Nations official once spoke to me indignantly about this general cowardice. 'The Pope,' he said, 'expresses doubts in an official document as to whether there is any connection between overpopulation and economic development. That is a way of questioning the Secretary General of the United Nations. If the latter replied: "Yes, there *is* a connection," everything might change. But he won't say it. Yet he thinks it!'

I mentioned guiding rules. I have just explained a few for the use of the civilized peoples of the West: *to give, to guide, to help.* There is another rule which is no less important: *to remain ourselves.* By that I mean to maintain and defend our common values. One of these is family planning. Europe has a common birth-rate and that birth-rate is low. Let us therefore stop making ourselves ridiculous by preaching natalism to poverty-stricken underdeveloped countries. Let us instead propose an ideal of a better life to them towards which they can strive when, with our help, they have emerged from poverty. The U.S.S.R., at bottom, is playing our game (technical progress, birth control, a bourgeois society). In less than a century Japan has learnt it. All the other countries can join in too, little by little. Birth control finds them still divided. In South Asia a left wing is taking shape. In South America a right wing is slowing the movement down. It is not for us to play the latter off against the former in the international assemblies. Numerical victory could never be ours. It would be a denial of the values which we have to offer to the rest.

The United Nations of 1945 were led by the Western states. Since then, Communist China has not been admitted to the organization, and if she did belong to it she would still have only one vote. In the New York secretariat the electoral system has got no further than the old property qualification—the states are represented according to their financial contribution. But in the internal evolution of the Western countries (which international evolution nowadays tends to reproduce) the property qualification was just a stage on the way to universal suffrage. The cry of 'One man, one vote' can be heard today in the depths of Central Africa. Perhaps it will be heard one day at the United Nations. Already the emancipation of Western colonies has given the Assembly an Afro-Asian majority which is influenced by the overpopulated states. This is an evolution which needs to be watched carefully, for in the long run it could lead to the breakdown of the present international system and a general degradation of civilization. But this is only the political aspect of the problem. The real game is being played on a different level. We (the West) have given up conquering and ruling. We propose simply to guide. We shall succeed in that if we can show that we are capable of solving certain human problems which face us today and will face everybody one day.

The industrial societies of today, through the extension of the period of education and increasing longevity, are moving gradually towards a form of existence of which the active part will be the briefest. This, for a country like the United States, is a prospect which is quite new and even revolutionary. It is unprepared for it. At present, active life colours the rest of existence. Children are directed, not according to their aspirations, but according to the demands of the economy which summons them. (Young students with a bent for literature devote themselves to mathematics which they hate.) Even leisure is monopolized by industry and devoted not to the development of personality but to the consumption of manufactured articles. Producers are encouraged to satisfy the easiest appetites and consumers to prefer objects which can be produced at decreasing cost. The result is the beginning of a robotizing process which everybody deplores and which nobody tries to arrest. This system will one day reach its limit. When everything has been inexorably regulated, when we have succeeded by dint of ingenuity in making men reduced to numbers live together, we shall come up against an unexpected resistance: that of apathy. 'Why should I bother?' the individual will ask. 'Nobody really cares any more about me.' The State will consequently obtain nothing but what it demands. Indeed I am wrong to talk about the future. This reaction already exists. It preoccupies the authorities in the Communist world as in the capitalist world.

One remedy is to infuse some interest into the dreary routine of the factory and the office (or into its extensions: trade union activities, etc.). But, as Georges Friedmann writes, 'this process of revaluation comes up against limits imposed by technique itself'. So it is chiefly outside organized work that we must look for the solution. Tomorrow the craftsman whom we flattered ourselves we had eliminated will reappear. He will paint, embroider, make furniture. But he will do all that *for his own pleasure*. Nobody will dishonour these tasks any more with the curt description: 'unprofitable'. The new science of cybernetics tries to fit men into economic programmes. Perhaps it will end up by distributing work, not according to the decisions of political leaders, the armament plans of states, or the requirements of productivity, but according to the workers' natural capacities and in conformity with *values* they have chosen. Even if it becomes much more flexible than it is at present, it will find this hard to achieve. If we ever attain that golden age, it will not be the man but the machine which will appear maladjusted.

In an interesting study, Joffre Dumazedier recalls that the length of the average working week in France has gone down in the past hundred years from seventy-five to forty-five hours; in other words, counting holidays with pay as well, an annual increase in free time of 1,500 hours. The worker tries in this free time to restore the human values banished from work by the disappearance of family enterprise and craftsmanship. During the whole of the nineteenth century, activities of no benefit to society were subjected to a sort of moral censure. They were placed under the heading of 'idleness', a pejorative expression. But for some time now the dictionary definitions of leisure have shown an evolution of the idea which investigations have confirmed. Leisure is no longer presented as a 'condition', nor even as a 'time', but as an 'occupation'. While work is going to sleep in the monotony of repetitive gestures, leisure is taking on (or should be taking on) an active character. In it a man can cleanse himself of the dirt left by organized time. Already, in opposition to the puritanical capitalist propaganda of the nineteenth century, most workers, even the skilled men (as the surveys show), regard leisure as the essential part of their life and try to protect it from the contagion of industrial work. Hence the popularity of camping, gardening, fishing. In other words, with their work people gain time which they then set out to lose again by plunging into the unattached time of old.

Our technocrats are alarmed at this evolution which tends to limit their powers. They defend themselves against it by claiming that it is technical progress which has made an extension of leisure possible. This argument is not unanswerable. Work which was less dehumanized, even at the cost of shorter leisure, might satisfy man's deeper aspirations better. But let us admit that it would be difficult to turn back the clock. We still have to agree that we obtain the reward of progress in the form of *real* freedom. The American consumer conditioned by big business and the Chinese indoctrinated by the State are deprived of this reward. In the United States (above a certain level) consumption no longer satisfies material needs, but a desire for prestige artificially created by industrial producers. The objects a man possesses assign him a rank in society. Games themselves are put to utilitarian purposes. The artistic part of a television programme is above all a prop for the commercial part. In the Communist countries, leisure is the slave, not of publicity, but of propaganda: this represents no progress whatever. Besides, the same problem faces all men: to take full advantage of their 'free time' they would have to have a moral equipment which they have lost. Cut off from Nature and tradition, and gorged on a succession of pictures, man risks having pleasures as poor as his work.

Left to itself, the Western economy would move ineluctably towards leisure in spite of all the efforts it makes to prevent itself from doing so. It is moving only slowly in that direction, for two reasons. Competition with the Communist world (so we are told) makes it impossible for it to slacken its pace. ('This is begging the question,' observes Pierre Drouin, 'for that competition concerns not just the standard of living but living *conditions*.') Its internal rivalries have the same effect. (In the race for expansion, France and Italy have just taken the lead over Germany and Britain because, unlike the last two countries, they have not reduced their working hours.) The general direction of the evolution is none the less certain.

In Europe the question of leisure is of particular interest to women. The forty-six-hour week now generally in force obliges them to sacrifice their home to their work. 'With a forty-hour week,' notes Roger Priouret, 'they would feel that they were better able to fulfil their role as mother and wife, which is the most important thing for them. In the United States, as we have seen, the desire for leisure is not as strong, but it will assert itself all the same, and probably more rapidly. If the West were to go on preferring gadgets to leisure, it would arrive at a ridiculous situation in which cars, television sets, records, transistors and other new machines would demand time from man which he would no longer be able to give them. Civilization would then have become "an insidious torture of Tantalus".'[28]

Just when we might begin preparing ourselves for the advancement of leisure, we are saddled with the task of feeding, clothing, and providing for a world population *increasing in geometrical progression.* Three forms of selfishness are concealed here behind the mask of generosity: the 'rabbitism' of the primitive peoples, the neurasthenia of the civilized,[29] the imperialism of the technocrats. The latter, for lack of an adequate humanist culture, do not know what real freedom is. Afflicted with poor sight (both sensual and spiritual), indifferent to the beauty of forms and colours as to the mysteries of the world, they try to extend their infirmity to the whole of mankind. In the noise and agitation which they foster, concentration becomes more difficult, antennae atrophy. We can no longer even see what we lack. To increase *doing*, the better to bury *being*—that is the conspirators' sinister programme.

In a book by the American economist Rostow (one of President Kennedy's advisers) I find this question: 'Shall we find a way of destroying capital without destroying the world so as to be able to go on working?' That is how a technocrat sees the future: we must at all costs 'go on working'. And for that purpose, if need be, 'destroy capital'. The progressives are entitled to reply that it would be better to use that capital to finance proliferation. But that is just another way of refusing any improvement of the human condition. Our so-called progressives do not dare to attack creative leisure openly; but they speak of it only with conventional phrases which barely conceal their contempt, and try to ruin everything which could give it value. They have in fact entered into a strange alliance with the backward peoples of the world, with a view to forcing the most highly developed section of mankind to abandon its cultural conquests and to use its skill and knowledge to build an ant-hill.

Pierre George has written an interesting study of the magical effects of numbers. The sight of a great quantity of men is naturally impressive, but if they are turned into a *mass* the effect is terrifying. The Chinese will soon number a *a milliard.* A figure (of hundreds of millions) reduced in this way to a single unit is, as it were, multiplied again. The distinctions which might induce one to break it down in order to preserve the complexity of reality are eliminated. We are never told and do not know the number of *adequately fed* Chinese or of *educated* Chinese. If these headings were created, Great China would become small, the myth would collapse. Instead, we cling to a simplification which fosters a collective delirium.

A detailed study needs to be made of the subtle degradations of culture caused by the proliferation of human beings. While the nobler meanings of the word 'democracy' are weakened, others gain new strength. The law of the majority assets itself brutally, without troubling any longer about the rights of minorities or about respect for the individual. From democracy, by way of demography, we are sliding towards demagogy. In schools swamped with children, the teaching is for the last rather than the first. (It would be better to try to create a new aristocracy, more valid and more open than those of birth and wealth.) In the world of research, subjects which cannot be reduced to numerical terms are treated numerically, and electronic machines are asked questions which they can answer easily, even though their answers are valueless if the questions they are asked are not the right ones. In this way false ideas develop with certain dangerous consequences which the Americans are beginning to realize.[30]

An excessively high rate of reproduction fosters and accentuates these dangers. Technique and numbers then form an unholy alliance. Together, they create a prison from which man, in the long run, would no longer be able to escape except in the event of a regressive cataclysm. In China, I felt as if I were visiting that prison. Quantity and quality there had become indistinguishable. I explained how I felt one day to some Communists who were showing me round a cultural club in Shanghai, and I reproduce here my remarks as I noted them down at the time: 'What frightens me is what I read in your newspapers: the leader writer who proposes as models men who have "studied less, but mixed with the people more"; the pupil who claims to have succeeded in equalling his absent master's knowledge in forty-eight hours' intensive study; the peasant-woman who prides herself on having written ten thousand lines without stopping; and the worker who, having already written six novels and 483 poems in the course of the year, announces his intention of stepping up his production. Intellectuals can regard all this only as an insult to their professional conscience.'[31] I imagine that most of my readers will share my reaction. Yet are we not already pursuing the same course? Have we, too, not got our literary record holders? Before television programmes are planned, viewing figures are obtained. This is tantamount to asking for instructions from a majority of ordinary people which is incapable of giving them and indeed wants to receive them. An entirely different attitude should be adopted. The history of culture is full of discoveries made by a few which have later enriched many. But this diffusion of quality is possible only in a certain atmosphere of creative freedom which is dangerously threatened today.

In a book signed by a famous name (and full of interesting observations) I find this brief equation: 'Organization + Technique = Culture.'[32] What blasphemy! True culture is precisely that which enables man to view technique and organization in proper perspective, to put them in their places, to prevent these servants from turning into tyrants. To say that technique can create values is to misunderstand the very nature of the latter. They spring from a free affirmation of the spirit, illuminated by a private revelation or guided by the example of inspired men in whom humanity has transcended itself. A green traffic light (which is cited as an example in the same book) tells us very usefully when we can cross a road, but not why we must go out or where we must go. Our technocrats, incidentally, have their own values, which are no more 'objective' than the rest. They often present, as inspired by purely rational considerations, economic plans which have been dictated by choices of a different order. (The creation of a metallurgical industry in a country poor in raw materials reflects a desire for independence or for power, not a desire to organize the economy within the context of an international division of labour or in the consumers' interests.) 'Realism' in such cases is just a catchword.

In China I saw men eat statistics. The newspaper reader was submitted every day to a process of hot and cold showers: records broken by the producer, bad news for the consumer. The good Communist found consolation for eating less rice and pork in the idea that he had produced more, without trying too hard to understand this contradiction. In point of fact, the statistics which encouraged him were false, but the same effect would have been produced by accurate statistics. In this case the Chinese would rightly have seen in his privations a moral act, a sacrifice of the present to the future; but this sacrifice would still have been a piece of trickery, for it would have been accepted in favour of a mythical successor. No appreciable improvement in the standard of living will occur as long as the country's savings continue to be absorbed by the increase in population.

If they set foot on this slippery slope, the technocrats will end up by encountering what in their eyes is the supreme humiliation: a *technical* failure. They set out to influence man, but their science is effective only with things. Already the body of the ageing man finds it hard to adjust itself to the continual conversions which increasingly rapid technical progress demands of him. The past which men would like to abolish lingers on in the subconscious, where psycho-analysis discovers it and from which brainwashing cannot manage to banish it. The family is hard to kill. Fathers and sons want to communicate, want to share their experience. They will no longer be able to do so if an accelerated evolution leaves them with no common language, and then both will suffer frustration. From all this human resistance there rises a cry which makes our technocrats smile: 'Slow down the acceleration of history!' 'Impossible!' they reply. Yet that desire will one day be shared by all mankind, and it is incumbent upon the élites of the old countries to go some way towards meeting it. Instead of passively waiting for economic development to give us a 'spiritual supplement', let us tackle all the things which despiritualize: overpopulation, Communism, advertising, the mechanization of the higher activities, the quantification of quality.

Here I must criticize—very regretfully—a certain philosophy whose intentions are extremely noble but which covers a great many misunderstandings. Teilhard de Chardin seems in his books to identify the complexification of organization with spiritual progress, collectivization with what he calls a 'noosphere'. The result is that readers who have not read him very attentively have a feeling of general satisfaction—the good technocrat believes that he has been given the absolution already earned by the good Christian. One might compare mankind today to a student sitting in front of a blackboard. He sees two rising curves on it: that of production, which raises his spirits, and that of overpopulation, which creates a certain feeling of anxiety. When he is told that the first can pull along the second indefinitely and that a third—the curve of spiritual progress—will come into line with these parallels, his fear disappears and a feeling of euphoria takes its place. I am afraid that a terrible awakening lies ahead.

For a glimpse of the future, let us turn again to those animal societies in which Merleau-Ponty looked for 'anticipatory caricatures of man'. Certain insects accept the presence of their congeners only up to a given level of tolerance. When this level has been passed, they change. For example, in certain climatic conditions (heavy rain, etc.) countless crickets are born, and then, very swiftly, the group *gregarizes*, or, in other words, begins to react as a whole with synchronized reflexes. Overpopulation produces morphological effects; the metabolism, the very appearance of the individuals are modified; the crickets change colour. 'Once the process has been set in motion', writes Marcel Sire, 'it grows like an explosive reaction which was just waiting for the spark. The grubs leave the gregarigenic centres, first walking, then jumping; the primary groups from these centres merge together when they meet, the biggest group leading the others. They move in a given direction, in a straight line which never goes round obstacles but over them, even if the obstacle is a river. They go forward like a battalion of sleepwalkers.' These blind migrants end up by meeting parasites or unfavourable living conditions. Then a fresh mutation occurs. They lose their green livery and return to their solitary form. After a *gregarization* of humanity, a transformation of the same sort would take place. We would end up by starting once again from scratch, in the isolation of the first men.

For a long time I believed that we could expect corrective action from governments, international organizations, official bodies. I have lost this illusion. The essential questions are put in a carefully preserved vacuum. The moral and political authorities, intimidated by active minorities, will remain incapable of controlling the unleashed forces of world demography unless some new force intervenes. It is therefore essential for the independent intellectual to come forward alone to the front of the stage.

What can he do with his tiny resources? He can fill people with a sense of urgency. One day, being driven by a black chauffeur through an overpopulated territory, I asked how many brothers and sisters he had. He answered me by listing them, then, having recalled them in that way and keeping them before his eyes, he counted them up and arrived at the total: eleven. Mankind is in the process of performing on a larger scale the operation which I had just accidentally launched in a single family. One of the intellectual's first tasks is, in fact, to help mankind to count itself—and also to teach it to count together only elements which are comparable. If the underdeveloped peoples want to enjoy the whole of our civilization, they must accept not only part of it (medical progress and financial aid) but its entirety (including birth control, savings, and education).

The intellectual has an even loftier task, which is to speak to all men, through the more intelligent among them, to say to them:

'The ageing of mankind has become ineluctable. To avoid it in spite of the reduction in mortality which (happily) is taking place, there would have to be an increase in the birth-rate which would undoubtedly produce a general catastrophe. We must therefore adjust ourselves to this ageing and discover the opportunities it offers us. The old natural process, in which men followed one another swiftly, carried off by murderous conflicts or natural cataclysms without having exhausted their potentialities, is going to be replaced—if civilization survives—by a slower process, with more enlightened men, who will strive less fiercely with one another. We are moving *in any case* towards a new demographic equilibrium, but it is a question of finding out at what level and by what methods. An immediate braking would fix the provisional ceiling of the world population towards the end of the century at a reasonable level, allowing for moderate growth later on. If we begin by passing that level, a process of *depopulation* will be necessary to return to it. The hour of decision is approaching. We shall have to decide, either to give up unborn children, or to destroy or degrade living human beings. The problem is unavoidable, but the choice of victims is ours.

'In any event, there will one day be six milliard inhabitants on this earth. But they must not be doomed to expect twelve milliard, who would crush them. Let us instead thin out the future crop, as the woodcutter thins out the forest in order to allow the saplings room to grow. And above all, let us try to make life worth living for those who are to be summoned to it. Let us set them a pattern of life which they can follow and give them assistance in lifting themselves up to it. This operation of charm (which the Communists will call corruption) may tomorrow be the West's principal weapon of defence. But it will also benefit all men. They are short, not only of food, but of knowledge; they are thirsty for education as well as water. We owe them these benefits.'

Six milliard insects? I still hope for six milliard men.

Notes

1. In 1961 Tunisia, a Moslem country, authorized the opening of birth-control clinics on its territory. Pakistan had already authorized them and has now embarked on a considerable propaganda campaign for contraception. Nasser in his turn has just declared himself in favour of birth control. Is this an effect of the resistance put up by the granite of Aswan to the Soviet engineers?

The Spanish birth-rate has risen during recent years to 22 per 1,000 in 1957–60, a figure which is still distinctly inferior to the birth-rate in the United States during the same period (25 per 1,000).

2. This is not even certain. After an atomic war the world might find itself relatively more overpopulated than before, the regression of technical civilization being even more pronounced than the diminution of the number of human beings.

3. Ten inhabitants per hectare.

4. S. Chandrasekhar, in his book *Population and Planned Parenthood in India*, quotes two documents which it is interesting to compare. Queen Victoria wrote to the King of the Belgians in 1841: 'I think, dearest Uncle, you cannot really wish me to be the *maman d'une nombreuse famille*, for I think you will see with me the great inconvenience a *large family* would be to us all, and particularly to myself.' But in 1878, during the reign of the same sovereign, the Governor of Bombay, Sir Richard Temple, urged by a local potentate to take steps 'to restrain in some measure at all events, the inordinate aptitude of the people to increase the population', indignantly replied that he 'would do everything in his power for the increase, and nothing for the diminution, of Her Majesty's subjects'.

5. Closer investigation would reveal a few differences between the Marxist doctrinaires. Engels was not as impervious as Marx to

demographic preoccupations. Kautsky made a distinction between absolute overpopulation (in relation to resources) and relative overpopulation (in relation to institutions).

6. The same preoccupation exists in the U.S.S.R. In June 1962, at the Warsaw Family Planning Congress, Moscow announced the discovery of a Soviet oral contraceptive superior to that of the United States. Between the two great powers, after the race for the 'absolute weapon', the race for the 'absolute pill' has begun.

7. While correcting the proofs of this book I have just learnt of two important modifications of Communist policy: China has resumed her contraceptive propaganda and the U.S.S.R. has just admitted an initial contingent of Chinese workers to Siberia. It is too early yet to appreciate the scope of this news.

8. There is a lot of talk about the population-subsistence ratio. Something ought to be said about the population-education ratio. According to a report by the U.N.E.S.C.O. Secretariat published in 1962, half the world's inhabitants are still illiterate. Worse still, between 1950 and 1960, in spite of the enormous educational effort made, an increase in the number of illiterates has been recorded.

9. In New Delhi differently coloured necklaces were distributed to Indian women to help them to distinguish between fertile and unfertile days. Many of them thought that it was sufficient for them to handle these necklaces to start a safe period.

10. This was promptly interpreted in two opposite ways: some asserted that it was a symptom of androgynization, others that female moustaches are particularly luxuriant in Puerto Rico.

11. The period immediately preceding the appearance of the sign would, however, remain uncertain on account of the survival of spermatozoons in the female organs.

12. Percentage comparisons between the rhythm method and 'artificial methods' have little value, for it would be necessary to begin by fixing the exact duration assigned to the so-called 'safe period'. Because of the considerable irregularity of feminine cycles, only lengthy abstinence every month makes a satisfactory degree of safety possible. Few couples seem capable of conforming with such a stringent

requirement. The rhythm method *as it is usually practised* gives less favourable results than the other methods.

13. According to other American surveys, the pill would seem to produce a slight reduction of the *libido*. In France, Dr. Lagroua Weill-Hallé has noted the contrary effect. In these delicate matters observation may unconsciously reflect the personal opinions of the observer (or the special characteristics of his clients).

14. According to a survey carried out in the Puerto Rican districts in New York, mechanical and chemical contraceptives are the object of various pejorative legends which lazy couples cite as a pretext for not using them. These couples (usually recent immigrants) end up by applying for sterilization. There is less enthusiasm for sterilization and less contempt for mechanical and chemical contraception among couples who have been established in New York for some time.

15. *Constellation*, No. 168.

16. There could be a different interpretation: namely that intellectuals are more hypocritical. I am ignoring this unflattering hypothesis.

17. This figure is obviously just an average. But it corresponds to the desires of a vast majority of individual families.

18. This is why many Frenchwomen threatened with illegitimate or inopportune births go to Switzerland. But it seems that there is a flow in the opposite direction, from Switzerland to France. A woman prefers to have an abortion in a place where she is not known.

19. The State of Madras pays a bonus of thirty rupees to any man who allows himself to be sterilized, and pays the fee of the surgeon who performs the operation. Mobile surgical teams are now being organized. Dr. Chandrasekhar, the eminent Indian demographer, writes to me on the subject: 'We consider that the cost of the operation and the bonus is lower in the long run than the cost to the State of unwanted children.'

20. We often hear of the desire peasants are supposed to have for a large number of male children in order to have cheap agricultural labour at their disposal as soon as possible. It would appear from various surveys that this state of mind is now relatively rare. Similarly *machism*, which we have mentioned, is definitely in decline.

21. The West also has to combat partial and regional underdevelopment within its own area.

22. Paradoxically, this is often very considerable in underdeveloped areas. United Nations experts consider it one of their successes that they have persuaded the inhabitants of a few overpopulated areas of South Asia to cut down their wedding festivities.

23. *Pamphlet*, 12 May 1933.

24. When all the Customs barriers between the Common Market countries have been abolished who is going to stop contraceptive products from entering France?

25. 'The doctor has no function to fulfil and no responsibility to assume in the application of contraceptive methods, or in the giving of advice or demonstrations on the use of these methods. The doctor has no right to use his professional capacity as a surety for the activities of these Family Planning Centres.' (*Presse médicale*, 3 February 1962.)

26. In the United States, the number of white wives who are sterile has fallen from 17 per cent to 10 per cent between 1950 and 1955. In a group of sterile women examined recently, only 4 per cent were voluntarily sterile, whereas that proportion reached 40 per cent in a group examined between 1927 and 1940 by the Indianapolis survey.

27. In Latin America a certain resignation to wife-desertion and illegitimacy co-exists with absolute opposition to birth control. Writers who see in this an implicit cruelty have spoken of 'unchristian Catholics'. This Latin-American state of mind is probably destined to change.

28. Pierre Drouin, *Le Monde*, 16 May 1962.

29. Overpopulation, by means of the work it creates, acts as a *diversion* (in the Pascalian meaning of the word).

30. The military technicians of the United States recently realized that the American defence system had been directed in accordance with arbitrary hypotheses, chosen 'to please the machines'.

31. *Le Monde en 1960*.

32. Louis Armand, the author of *Plaidoyer pour l'avenir*, has told me, in a conversation after this book was written, that this formula, taken out of its context, does not entirely express his meaning. I am happy to record this comment. I should have been very sorry to find myself in direct disagreement with this eminent, warm-hearted man.

Bibliography

ARMAND, Louis, and DRANCOURT, Michel: *Plaidoyer pour l'avenir.* Calmann-Levy (Paris, 1961).

ARON, Raymond: *Paix et guerre entre les nations.* Calmann-Levy (Paris, 1962).

BENNETT, Merril K.: *The World's Food.* Harper and Brothers (New York, 1954).

BERGUES, Helene: *La prévention des naissances dans la famille.* Presses Universitaires de France (Paris, 1960).

BOUNOURE, L.: *Reproduction sexuelle et histoire naturelle du sexe.* Flammarion (Paris, 1947).

BOUTHOUL, Gaston: *Sauver la Guerre.* B. Grasset (Paris, 1962).

BUQUET, Léon: *Cours de démographie.* Les Cours de Droit (Paris, 1959).

CHANDRASEKHAR, S.: *Population and Planned Parenthood in India.* Allen and Unwin (London, 1955).

CHEN, Kuan: *World Population Growth and Living Standards.* Twayne (New York, 1960).

CHEVALIER, Louis: *Problèmes de la population.* 3 vols. Les Cours de Droit (Paris, 1950).

COALE, Ausley: *Population Growth and Economic Development in Low Income Countries.* Oxford University Press (India, 1958).

COOKE, Robert C.: *Human Fertility: the Modern Dilemma.* Gollancz (London, 1951).

DUBOS, René: *Mirage of Health.* Allen and Unwin (London, 1960).

DUMAZEDIER, Joffre: *Vers une civilization du loisir.* Le Seuil (Paris, 1962).

DUMONT, R. *Types of Rural Economy.* Methuen (London, 1957).

DUNN, Halbert L.: *Significance of Levels of Wellness in Ageing.*

DUVERGER, Maurice: *Cours de sociologie politique*. Les Cours de Droit (Paris, 1962).

FOURASTIE, Jean: *Histoire de demain*. Presses Universitaires de France (Paris, 1956). *La Civilization en 1975*. Presses Universitaires de France (Paris, 1953).

FREEDMAN, Ronald: *Family Planning, Sterility and Population Growth*. McGraw-Hill (New York, 1959).

FRIEDMANN, Georges: *Anatomy of Work*. Heinemann (London, 1961). *Où va le travail humain*. Gallimard (Paris, 1950).

GOTTMANN, Jean: *Megalopolis*. Twentieth Century (New York, 1961).

HAUSER, P. M.: *Population and World Politics*. Free Press (Chicago, 1958).

HIMES, Norman: *The Truth about Birth Control*. John Day (New York, 1931).

JACOBS, Jane: *The Death and Life of Great American Cities*. Jonathan Cape (London, 1962).

KEYNES, J. M.: *Essays in Biography*. Rupert Hart-Davis (3rd edit.) (London, 1951).

LESTAPIS, S. de: *Family Planning and Modern Problems*. Burns Oates (London, 1961).

MCCLEARY, G. F.: *Malthusan Population Theory*. Faber and Faber (London, 1953).

MACURA, Milos: *La population de la Yougoslavie et ses conditions de développement*. Institut National d'études démographiques (Paris, 1955).

MEIER, Richard L.: *Modern Science and the Human Fertility Problem*. Chapman and Hall (London, 1959).

MICHAEL, Donald N.: *Cybernation: the Silent Conquest*.

MOUSSA, Pierre: *Underprivileged Nations*. Sedgwick and Jackson (London, 1962).

MUMFORD, Lewis.: *The Culture of Cities*. Secker and Warburg (London, 1940).

MYRDAL, Gunnar: *International Economy*. Routledge & Kegan Paul (London, 1956).

NELSON, Warren O.: *Current Research in the Regulation of Fertility*.

OSER, Jacob: *Must Men Starve?* Jonathan Cape, (London, 1956).

PADILLA, Gunnar: *Up from Puerto Rico*. University of Columbia Press (New York, 1958).

RAINWATER, Lee: *And the Poor get Children*. Quadrangle Books (Chicago, 1960).

RUSSELL, Sir E. John: *World Population and World Food Supplies*. Allen and Unwin (London, 1954).

SANGER, Margaret: *An Autobiography*. Gollancz (London, 1939).

SAUVY, Alfred: *La montée des Jeunes*. Calmann-Levy (Paris, 1959). *La population*. Presses Universitaires de France (Paris, 1944). *L'Europe et sa population*. Editions Internationales (Paris, 1953). *Théorie générale de la population*. Presses Universitaires de France (Paris, 1952–5). *Le Tiers-Monde*. Presses Universitaires de France (Paris, 1961). *Richesse et population*. Payot (Paris, 1943). *Fertility and Survival, Population Problems from Malthus to Mao-Tse-Tung*. Chatto & Windus (London, 1961).

SCHEINFELD, Amram: *You and Heredity*. Chatto & Windus (London, 1952).

SIRE, Marcel: *La vie sociale des animaux*. Le Seuil (Paris, 1960).

SPENGLER, J.: *Population theory and Policy*. Free Press (Chicago, 1956).

SUTTER, S.: *L'eugenique*. Presses Universitaires de France (Paris, 1950).

TAEUBER, Irène: *The Changing Population of the United States*. Chapman & Hall (London, 1958). *Asia's Increasing Population*.

TIETZE, Christopher: *The Clinical Effectiveness of Contraceptive Methods. Legal Abortion in Eastern Europe*.

VIRALLY, Michel: *L'O.N.U. d'hier à demain*. Le Seuil (Paris, 1961).

VOGT, William: *Challenge to Survival*. Gollancz (London, 1961).

WEILL-HALLÉ, Dr. Lagroua: *La libre conception à l'étranger*. Maloine (Paris, 1959). *Contraception orale ou locale*. Maloine (Paris, 1962).

WHYTE, William H., Jr.: *The Organization Man*. Jonathan Cape (London, 1957).

WOODHAM SMITH, Cecil: *The Reason Why*. Constable (London, 1953).

PERIODICALS

Population (France).

Population Studies (U.K.).

Population Bulletin (U.S.A.).

Bulletin S.E.D.E.I.S.

REPORTS

UNITED STATES

Reports of the White House Conference on Ageing: (*The Nation and its Older People*), (*Ageing in the States*), (*Ageing with a Future*).

Annual report 1959, University of Puerto Rico.

UNITED KINGDOM

Report of the Royal Commission on Population (*London, 1949*). H.M.S.O., 1950, 5 vols.

INDIA

Report of the Sixth International Conference on Planned Parenthood (*1959*).

FRANCE

Rapport de la Commission d'étude des problèmes de la vieillesse: politique de la vieillesse.

UNITED NATIONS

Development through Food.

Community Development and Economic Development.

L'accroissement démographique et le niveau de vie dans le pays sous-développes.